CARNATIONS AND PINKS

As a past president of the British National Carnation Society and an expert and successful grower of carnations and pinks for many years, F. R. McQuown is particularly well placed to pass on the knowledge which is essential to achieve first-class results. Mr McQuown has the ability, rare among writers, of being able to explain complex physical processes and technicalities connected with growing plants so that these immediately come into sharp focus in the reader's mind.

Logically and systematically he follows his discourse on the types of carnations and pinks with details of how these plants should be grown in greenhouse or garden. Propagation and breeding are given considerable attention, as one would expect from an author who has for years treated plant breeding as an absorbing hobby. Numerous pinks of his raising, almost all with the prefix 'London', have been introduced into commerce. Many of his varieties have also been given high awards by the Royal Horticultural Society.

Carnations and Pinks

F. R. McQUOWN, M.A., F.L.S.

(Past President of the British National Carnation Society)

THE GARDEN BOOK CLUB
121 CHARING CROSS ROAD, LONDON W.C.2

First Published in 1965
by W. H. & L. Collingridge Limited
Tower House, Southampton Street, London W.C.2
© *F. R. McQuown*

Acknowledgement

I wish to express my gratitude and thanks to Mr S. L. Lord, Garden Superintendent of the Shenley Hospital, Past President of the British National Carnation Society, for his great help and numerous suggestions, especially concerning growing under glass. Although I alone take responsibility for what is written in this book, I should not have undertaken to write it without his great experience behind me.

F. R. McQ.

Printed in Great Britain by
Morrison & Gibb Limited
London and Edinburgh

Contents

Illustrations

PHOTOGRAPHS

Between pages 32 and 33

A self border carnation
Border carnations
Border carnations
Dark-centred perpetual-flowering carnation blooms
Double pinks (author)
A laced pink (author)
A single pink
Exhibition group of laced pinks (author)
Typical blooms of perpetual-flowering carnations (author)
Perpetual-flowering carnations of informal shape
Rooted layer of border carnation (author)
Rooted cuttings of perpetual-flowering carnations (author)
Rooted cuttings of pinks (author)
A group of annual carnation blooms
Wisley trials of border carnations (author)
Raised bed in large carnation house (author)
Ground bed in large carnation house (author)
Bed shown in previous photograph in bloom

LINE DRAWINGS

by Dora Ratman

Chapter One

Types of Carnations and Pinks

Many people fail or are disappointed in their first attempts to grow carnations and pinks because they get a type of plant which is unsuitable for their purpose. Although they all belong to the genus *Dianthus*, there are three main types of carnation, and the correct ways of growing them are as different as the methods for growing, for example, roses, orchids and zinnias. There is some similarity between border carnations and pinks, but their cultivation is not quite the same.

It should be noted that the Royal Horticultural Society uses four different committees of experts to judge carnations and pinks, which is a record for one genus (see page 12). Thus this book is really about four entirely different kinds of plant (though in a general flower show all the carnations would probably be classified as one 'kind' of plant). It is obvious that unless the distinctions are made clear at the outset, a hopeless muddle will result.

Although this is a strictly practical book, it is much easier to understand and remember the differences between the various kinds of carnations and pinks if their history is considered.

Origin of Carnations. The word 'carnation' was originally applied to the wild plant *Dianthus caryophyllus*, a native of Europe, particularly France. The name is derived ultimately from the Latin word *corona*, meaning a 'chaplet, garland or crown', and originally was sometimes spelled 'coronation'. Incidentally, much confusion has arisen because there is another word 'carnation' in English (derived from a Latin word for 'flesh') meaning 'flesh-pink'. This word, which is seldom used nowadays, has of course nothing to do with the flower.

The flowers of *Dianthus caryophyllus* are small, single, and usually magenta or red in colour, but the colour is very variable. This plant was much cultivated in gardens, probably because of its strong clove scent, and it is often included in old paintings. It seems that double forms appeared a long time ago. Some can be seen, for example, in the painting *The Merchant* by Holbein (1497–1543). This painting, by the way, is so accurate that it is possible to estimate roughly how long the blooms had been open when they were painted (the reader should be able to do this when he has finished reading this book).

In the course of time, the original carnations developed, through selection and later deliberate breeding, until early in the nineteenth century they attained the form and colouring which we know today.

BORDER CARNATIONS

As would be expected from the name, these carnations are intended for growing in the open border, being derived from the original hardy carnations. They have attained a perfection of form and colouring that is equalled by few plants. The size of the bloom is usually $2\frac{1}{4}$ to $3\frac{1}{4}$ inches across, the petals are broad and smooth-edged, and the flower is flat and circular.

Although border carnations are frost-hardy, they vary a lot in their tolerance of excessive wet. Some varieties, often favoured by exhibitors, are really only suitable for growing in pots in a cold greenhouse, where watering can be controlled. These varieties do not always do well outdoors, though in good seasons they may do so. A good nurseryman will always give advice on which of the two types a variety belongs to, and, when ordering, the beginner should say whether outdoor or greenhouse types are required.

Many people regard scent as very important, but others are prepared to do without it in order to get the greatest perfection of form and colour. It is seldom that both go together, and yellow varieties (so far) have no scent. Again, the nurseryman should be told if scent is required.

Border carnations need a winter rest, and do not do well in climates where there is not at any rate a little frost in the winter to check growth. In the spring, a young plant sends up one centre shoot, which carries a number of side shoots, each of which bears a bloom, and there is a bloom at the top of the centre shoot called the 'crown' bloom. It is most important that the centre shoot should not be damaged, and it must never be 'stopped' or pinched out, or a season's bloom will be lost.

While the centre shoot is growing and flowering, a number of side growths are produced near the bottom. These can be used for propagation, or they can be left to produce flowering shoots the next year.

Thus a border carnation, propagated in July and planted out

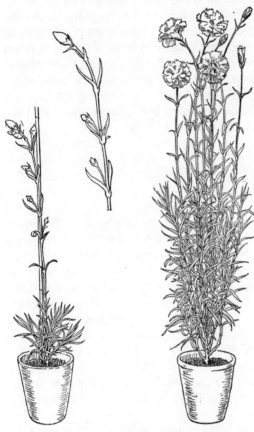

Left: Border carnation —note single central stem with side growths. Not yet disbudded

Centre: Same stem disbudded

Right: Perpetual-flowering carnation. Note taller growth, several stems, each disbudded to one bloom

the following September, will produce one flowering stem the following July, bearing up to half a dozen or so blooms on a stem about 2 feet long. The stems of the side blooms are rather short, and to get a fair length of stem on the crown bloom, some side stems will have to be sacrificed. There is no effective way of hastening the blooming by more than a few weeks. Nevertheless, the plant is popular because of the perfection of the blooms, for there is scarcely any plant in cultivation which approaches it in refinement of form and colour.

PERPETUAL-FLOWERING CARNATIONS

The perpetual-flowering carnation is so named because it has no resting period, growing continuously and rapidly, so that, if desired, a small collection of them can be kept perpetually in bloom. In practice, most people do not desire to keep them perpetually in bloom, but adjust their cultivation to get a crop of bloom at times of the year when flowers are scarce—for example, in the winter.

The perpetual-flowering carnation is a comparative newcomer, roughly dating from about the middle of the nineteenth century. There is no certainty about its origin, but it seems likely that the French *remontant* carnations played an important part in its parentage. Some expert growers consider that *Dianthus chinensis*, a species from the Far East which has given the present cultivated Indian pinks, figures in the ancestry of the perpetual-flowering carnation.

These are the carnations of the flower shops, and the popular name is 'hothouse carnations', though, as will be seen, the greenhouses in which they are grown are far from being what most people would call 'hot'. When they first appeared, border carnation enthusiasts refused to recognise them as worthy of the name of carnations, and for many years there were two national societies in England, one devoted to each type of plant. Both societies have now amalgamated to form the British National Carnation Society, but the society still maintains separate committees to deal with each of these two kinds of carnation, and a third committee to deal with pinks. Similarly, the Royal Horticultural Society has separate joint committees for each of these three kinds of flower, and annual carnations are dealt with by a fourth committee.

Temperatures for perpetual-flowering carnations. Although some varieties of perpetual-flowering carnation are frost-hardy, and are sometimes grown in cold greenhouses, the usual way of growing them is in a heated greenhouse. In order to get bloom in the winter, a normal night temperature of about 7° C. (45° F.) in winter is a suitable one for the beginner, though some people use as low as 5° C. (40° F.) or as high as 10° C. (50° F.). Commercial growers sometimes use higher temperatures for short periods, but this requires some skill if trouble is to be avoided. If, owing to exceptionally severe weather, or a failure of the heating system, the night temperature falls temporarily below 5° C. (40° F.), even perhaps below freezing point, the plants slow down. However, they usually make up by producing extra blooms when it gets warmer.

In contrast to border carnations, these plants require stopping; that is to say, the centre shoot is broken off. Disbudding is severe, only the top or crown bloom being allowed to develop on each shoot that is allowed to flower. Thus perpetual-flowering carnations have long stems to the blooms, and the blooms are mostly larger than those of border carnations. The early varieties, and most present-day ones, have indented edges to the petals, which are more numerous than in border carnations.

Types of perpetual-flowering carnation. There are two types of perpetual-flowering carnation. The one seen in the flower shops is the commercial type, and blooms very freely, with flowers 3 inches or rather more in diameter. The petals have indented or fringed edges, for these travel better in the boxes in which they are sent to market. The other, the exhibition type, often flowers less freely, but has much larger flowers, sometimes 4 or 5 inches across. There are, curiously enough, many people who have never seen an exhibition perpetual-flowering carnation. The exhibition type is grown by amateurs and specialist nurserymen, and since they do not have to be packed in boxes, the blooms often have smooth or nearly smooth edges to the petals.

Since they sell better, most commercial varieties are of one even colour, called 'selfs'. The exhibition varieties are mostly selfs, but there are some with intricate markings and blends of colour.

Some varieties are scented, and some are not. There are different scents among the scented varieties; some having the clove scent associated with border carnations, and some having a distinct and refreshing scent which is found only in perpetual-flowering carnations and some pinks. Occasionally there are other and fainter scents. Any of the scents may occur in either commercial or exhibition types.

Growth of perpetual-flowering carnations. Stopping the young plants results in branching close to the ground, and some of these branches are again stopped to ensure a continuity of bloom.

The growths for further blooming are produced for about a foot or so up from the bottom of the old flower stem; thus, as the plant grows older it gets taller and taller, and most amateurs do not grow a plant for more than two years.

Perpetual-flowering carnations grow much faster than border carnations. Exactly how long it would take to get the first possible bloom from a cutting would depend on the time of year, but the usual practice is to strike cuttings from December to March. This results in well-formed plants coming into bloom the following September to October.

Much conflicting information is published about the number of blooms per year produced by a plant, and there are various reasons for this. For example, commercial growers do not plant to get the greatest number of blooms per plant, but the greatest number of blooms for a given area of bed. Moreover, fuel is a small item for the commercial grower compared to overheads and labour, so it may pay him to use more heat, though the greater the heat the greater the skill needed.

The year is usually calculated from the beginning of flowering —September or October in most cases. This is a time when there are often large flushes of bloom, so a week or two's difference in the timing could include an extra flush, and inflate the figures.

All in all, the beginner can reasonably expect about seventeen to twenty blooms in a year from free-flowering varieties. Those with enormous blooms usually produce a much smaller number, even below half a dozen, so the beginner must decide whether he wishes to have many moderate-sized blooms or fewer large ones, and order his plants accordingly.

ANNUAL CARNATIONS
The third kind of carnation is the annual carnation, also called the marguerite carnation or Chabaud carnation. Strictly speaking, the annual carnations are half-hardy perennials, but they are treated as half-hardy annuals. Their cultivation is the same as that of such plants as stocks, china asters, petunias and the like.

Seed is sown in gentle heat early in the year, and in due course they are pricked out in boxes, hardened off and then planted out-doors. They bloom the same year, and on the approach of winter they are pulled up and discarded. If they are compared to other bedding plants, they are remarkably good, flowering freely and continuously and producing good blooms.

The true carnation enthusiast, however, looks down on annual carnations. This is because their flowers are markedly inferior to those of both border and perpetual carnations. When the Royal Horticultural Society tested a number of commercial strains of seed of these plants at the Wisley Gardens a short time ago, they were not judged by the regular carnation committees, but by the Floral A committee, which deals with garden plants generally.

Nevertheless, annual carnations are good plants, and are popular with many people. If they were not overshadowed by their famous relations they would no doubt be considered first class.

CLASSIFICATION OF CARNATION FLOWERS

Exhibitors of border carnations divide their blooms into classes according to the type of marking they show, and these classes are useful in describing the flower in catalogues, etc. Although these classes strictly apply only to border carnations, there is no reason why they should not be applied to any carnation as a convenient method of description, and catalogues often do so.

There is no reason why any particular colour marking should be associated with ease or difficulty of growing. There is, however, an apparent exception to this rule, and it will be mentioned under the appropriate heading. There are three main headings, namely selfs, fancies, and picotees, and these are set out below with their sub-divisions.

Selfs are of one even colour throughout. This class is subdivided according to the colour, such as white, scarlet, apricot, etc. Nearly all annual carnations, and most perpetual-flowering carnations, are selfs.

Where two or more colours occur in the bloom, it is described as a **fancy** (unless it is a picotee, described on page 15). The colours may blend, or there may be sharply defined markings of one or more colours on an even ground colour. Fancies are divided into white ground fancies, yellow ground fancies, and other fancies. The slightest trace of yellow or apricot classes the bloom as a yellow ground fancy.

During the last century, there were carnations known as 'flakes' and 'bizarres'. These had to have a pure white ground, and the markings were wedge-shaped. If the markings were all of one colour they were flakes, whereas bizarres had markings of two or more colours. If any existed now they would be classed as white ground fancies. Recently this type of marking has appeared again, but so far without the white ground. They are, however, often called flakes and bizarres.

Picotees can have a ground colour of white, yellow or buff, and the contrasting colour is in a band round the edge of the petal. If the band is very thin, it is a wire-edged picotee, whereas if the band is $\frac{1}{8}$ inch to $\frac{1}{4}$ inch wide, it is called heavy-edged. Intermediate types are called medium-edged.

Picotees are an apparent exception to the rule that the strength and vigour of the plant is unrelated to the colour of the flower. The reason is that the perfect picotee rarely appears, and when it does the raiser tries to hang on to it, even if it does not grow too well. Therefore many picotees are of somewhat weak growth, and not easy for the beginner, but this does not apply to all of them.

Whatever the colour or colours, a carnation with a clove scent may be exhibited as a **clove**.

PINKS

The first question to be answered is 'What is a pink?' There are all sorts of ingenious theories about the origin of the word 'pink' as applied to a flower, but they all break down or become doubtful under close examination. Often they fail because the name of the flower is older than the word from which it is supposed to be derived. There seems to be a lack of evidence in the matter. However, it is worth noting that this flower was regarded as a symbol of great perfection, hence we have such phrases as 'the pink of perfection' or the colloquial 'in the pink'. The use of the word to describe a colour occurs much later, presumably because most of them had a pink colour, as they have today. Perhaps some of them were scarlet, leading to the description of the huntsman's coat as 'pink', but this is a guess.

Strictly, any member of the genus *Dianthus* might be called a pink, and at one time carnations were called 'clove-pinks', though it is doubtful if the word is ever used nowadays. In modern English, if the word 'pink' is used of a hybrid without any qualifying word, it is taken to mean a plant at any rate partly derived from *Dianthus plumarius*, a native of south-east Europe.

Much hybridising has gone on, but good garden pinks retain a lightness and daintiness which is quite distinct from a carnation. Because of the hybridisation between them, it may be difficult in theory to distinguish between a pink and a carnation. In practice, as in the case of good port and sherry, there is no doubt. If they are both bad enough, there probably is no difference.

Usually only nurserymen grow pinks wholly under glass. They do this with part of their stock, to get extra-early blooms and spread the propagating season. The vast majority of pinks in this country are grown in the open border even by exhibitors, and this is where they are intended to be grown. Their cultivation is very similar to that of border carnations outdoors, though they are easier to grow.

Two distinct types of growth in pinks. There is no need to specify that the varieties ordered should be suitable for outdoors, but there are two distinct types of pink. The older type, such as the famous variety Mrs Sinkins, grows like a border carnation, and throws up one central stem in the first year bearing the flowers, the side growths flowering a year later. This kind must not be stopped.

The more modern type is derived from a cross between a pink and a perpetual-flowering carnation, made by the late Montagu Allwood, and named after him *Dianthus allwoodii*. Though not so perpetual as a perpetual-flowering carnation, this type flowers two or even three times in a season in bursts like a hybrid tea rose. This type should be stopped, so it is important to make sure to which type a variety belongs.

Few pinks are scentless, and lack of scent is regarded as a serious defect. However, its intensity varies considerably, and the scent is of two kinds, corresponding to the two main kinds found in perpetual-flowering carnations. Thus if strong clove scent is required, it should be specified.

The attempt to get yellow into the ordinary good pink has not yet succeeded, though there are some yellow hybrids which as yet are rather rough. The colours are therefore various forms of white, pink and red.

Classification of pinks by type of flower. The main distinction is between singles and doubles. Unlike single carnations, which are

18 CARNATIONS AND PINKS

stiff and clumsy, single pinks are light and graceful, and some people prefer them.

With pinks (and this is not so with many plants), the exhibition standards set out ideals which are extremely close to the ideals of a good garden plant, and are worth studying. For example, stems and not blooms are specified, so a stem which is erect and dainty and has plenty of side blooms is preferred. Thus, too large a flower, which is not held upright, is heavily penalised. Incidentally, in the Wisley trials, where pinks are judged as garden plants, no staking is allowed.

The habit should be compact, and the flower stems should not exceed 18 inches. The calyx should not split. The outer petals should be flat, and be firm without being clumsy. The edges of the petals may either be smooth, or regularly serrated, and the flower should be regular in shape and circular in outline. The term 'serrated' is always used of pinks, but is not strictly correct. 'Indented' or 'cut' would be better.

There are four main classes of double pinks described in the following paragraphs. Selfs, bicolors and fancies may have either smooth or serrated petals, but laced pinks should have smooth-edged petals.

Selfs are of one colour throughout, though flowers with a small and inconspicuous mark at the base of each petal are also classed as selfs. The base of each petal in a **bicolor** has a blotch of a contrasting colour, so that the flower shows a sharp circular zone or 'eye' in the centre. In a **laced pink**, the coloured blotch at the base of the petal is extended in a narrow, even band near the edge, leaving a clear patch in the centre, known as the ground.

At one time laced pinks were the only ones eligible for exhibition, and the ground colour had to be white, but nowadays other grounds are permitted in laced pinks. This type of marking is hardly ever found in flowers other than pinks, though some polyanthus have a somewhat similar pattern. Formerly laced pinks were more difficult to grow than other pinks, but now they are just as easy as any, and some are very easy indeed.

Any pink which does not fall into the above three classes is a **fancy**, usually with speckles or stripes.

Single flowers should have five evenly spaced petals, which should meet or overlap slightly so that spaces do not show between them. The petals should either be quite flat or have a waved appearance. They can be selfs or bicolors, and have smooth or serrated petals. Unlike doubles, large flowers are desirable in singles. It is extremely difficult to breed good singles, and there are not many good varieties available. In show schedules, whether singles or doubles are required is specified, except in the case of laced pinks, which must be double.

MEANING OF VARIETY

The word 'variety' has different meanings according to the kind of plant. For example, a variety of sweet pea is a strain of seed which produces flowers of a definite colour and shape. A variety of annual carnation is a strain of seed which produces plants true to habit and size and shape of flower, but not usually true to colour.

The other carnations and pinks do not come true from seed, but they do come true from cuttings or layers as the case may be. With these, a variety nearly always means the sum total of all the plants produced by cuttings and layers from one outstanding seedling. Scientifically, all these plants are referred to as a 'clone' (it rhymes with 'tone'). Very occasionally one of the cuttings or layers suddenly produces entirely different flowers. This is known as a 'mutation' or 'sport', and may be the beginning of a new variety. Strictly, any seedling or mutation could be called a new variety, but it is only the outstanding ones which are worth naming and calling varieties.

Choosing a variety. Once the grower has made up his mind what he wants, the next thing is to get the plants. With carnations and pinks, unlike many other plants, it is not very helpful to give lists of varieties. The first reason is that, with such refined plants, individual preferences vary so much. The second is that there are so many varieties that each nurseryman lists only some of them. The third reason is that varieties tend to drop out of lists quickly when a better variety arrives. The fourth reason is the most important of all: namely, that plants of the same variety can vary greatly in health and vigour according to the source from which they come.

Fortunately, the problem is easily solved. One must choose a reputable specialist nurseryman, tell him what is wanted and rely on him to say which varieties are suitable. There are a number

of firms which specialise in carnations and pinks. Some sell only
border carnations and pinks, some perpetual-flowering carnations
only, and one or two all three. If varieties are chosen at flower
shows, a check should be made to see that they are suitable for
the purpose required.

Few carnation specialists sell annual carnation seed, but it is
listed by many reputable seedsmen.

It is folly to buy anything but the best. It is not always the
most expensive that are the best, but good stock cannot be very
cheap. Carnation specialists are honest men, but even if they were
not they would not spoil their reputations by selling bad plants.
Moreover, it costs no more to propagate a good variety than a
bad one, and no specialist would be foolish enough to clutter up
his nursery with bad varieties.

There are various natural species of dianthus which are known
as pinks, but a work on rock or alpine gardening should be consulted about these. There are also a number of hybrid dianthus of
which seed is sold. These hybrids may be annual, biennial or
perennial, and some are very attractive. Mostly they are easy to
grow, and as the seller indicates how they should be grown, it is
not proposed to deal with them in this book, as it would take
space better devoted to the more usual plants.

Chapter Two

Site, Soil and Plant Foods

Although this book deals with four different plants as far as cultivation is concerned, they have much in common which distinguishes their cultivation from that of other plants. Thus it will be found that although growing is, of course, very different in the open and under glass, the greenhouse kinds differ from other greenhouse plants in much the same way as the hardy kinds differ from other hardy plants.

For the sake of convenience this chapter is mainly devoted to the conditions required for good cultivation in the open ground, and the next chapter deals with design of greenhouses and the composition of soil for use under glass, but, owing to the basic similarities of the four plants, many of the principles are the same. To save repetition, the principles are not separately discussed in each chapter. Both chapters should therefore be read even if the grower intends to grow wholly in the open or wholly under glass.

In considering what follows, it should be remembered that the aim is to describe ideal conditions, but carnations and pinks frequently do well in conditions which are far from ideal. The beginner is therefore strongly advised to go ahead with the soil and situations that he has, and regard improvement as a long-term measure. Liming the soil, if necessary, is easily done, and it is no more difficult to apply a correct fertiliser than an incorrect one, so there is no reason for bad cultivation in these respects.

Basic requirements. Probably the most marked difference between carnations and pinks and other plants lies in their behaviour towards free lime in the soil. The great majority of plants grown in gardens are tolerant of lime, but do equally well and sometimes better in soils which are just on the acid side of the neutral point. A smaller group, which, however, includes some important plants such as rhododendrons, are intolerant of lime. There are very few plants indeed which prefer an alkaline soil, but carnations and pinks are among them. Although it is difficult to make an alkaline soil acid, it is, fortunately, easy to make an acid soil alkaline, by the addition of lime in some form.

Another essential is that there should be no stagnant moisture, either on the roots or the foliage. Damage to the roots normally occurs in winter, and an ill-drained site in the open may be masked by a winter of low rainfall. Thus, when trouble occurs, the cause may not be obvious. Damage to foliage can occur both in summer and in winter, and could be hidden by a long spell of dry weather. The remedy is a free flow of air, either outdoors or in the greenhouse as the case may be.

The third essential is that there shall be no forcing. Forcing for this purpose means stimulating growth when there is insufficient light for the growth to be healthy. Both heat, moisture and plant foods stimulate growth, but in most cases heat is more important. In the open, planting in too shady a position leads to forcing, as does overheating a greenhouse in dull weather. In a greenhouse, poor ventilation can have the same effect, and, of course, also tends to keep moisture on the leaves.

We can sum this up by saying that all four kinds of dianthus, when compared to most other plants outdoors or under glass, generally require a more alkaline soil, better drainage, less moisture on the leaves and more light in relation to heat. One of the main factors is a free circulation of air, for this reduces both excessive moisture and heat. This short statement really contains the key to perfect growing, but it cannot be denied that many people get very good results where conditions are far from perfect.

All our four plants are alike in requiring good drainage and a soil that is not acid, but they differ among themselves regarding the other two factors, i.e., moisture on the leaves, and light in relation to heat, and also, of course, frost hardiness, and this will now be considered.

Pinks. Of the four, pinks are the most tolerant of moisture on the leaves, and the least tolerant of excessive heat in relation to light. Thus they will stand the wet conditions found outdoors, and if they are attacked by any pest or disease, liquid sprays can be used. On the other hand, anything approaching forcing has most undesirable results. Nurserymen who grow them under glass, to get earlier blooms for shows and to spread the propagating season, use large houses with a great deal of permanent ventilation, and withhold water in dull weather to prevent too fast growth.

Fortunately, pinks will withstand far lower temperatures than are found in the British Isles, so they do well outdoors. It is interesting that this applies fully to those races of pinks which are partly descended from perpetual-flowering carnations.

Border carnations. Border carnations are rather a mixed lot. Some will withstand as much moisture on the foliage as pinks, but some exhibition kinds will not. All border carnations can be grown under glass, but those which are intolerant of wet do not do well in the open, so the wisdom of specifying which sort is required is obvious. All are frost-hardy.

They will stand slightly, but not much, more heat in relation to light than pinks, but if grown under glass there must be ample ventilation at all times. No artificial heat is used by amateurs, although some professionals use very gentle heat over a long period to time blooms for early shows.

Liquid sprays can be used if necessary.

Perpetual-flowering carnations. Perpetual-flowering carnations will stand much more heat in relation to light, and will grow in the winter. The borderline between healthy growth and forcing seems to be about 10° C. (50° F.) in dull winter light, and it is safer for the beginner to aim for a winter night temperature of 7° C. (45° F.). If the temperature runs up on a sunny day, there is light to balance it, and no forcing will take place. In some places in the extreme south of England, there is more light, and slightly higher temperatures are possible. Experts can use a slightly higher temperature than beginners in any case.

They are very intolerant of moisture remaining on the leaves, so a free circulation of air is very important. Liquid sprays should not be used if they can be avoided, and chemicals should be applied as dusts or preferably smokes or vapour. Perpetual-flowering carnations will stand some frost in dry conditions.

Annual carnations. In order to get early bloom, it is usual to sow annual carnations in gentle heat in January or February, and slight forcing in the young stage does no harm provided it is not excessive. After hardening off, they will stand ordinary summer wet outdoors, and liquid sprays can be used.

Since the stagnant water-level in most sites is much lower in summer than in winter, and annual carnations occupy the site only in summer, they will often flourish in less well-drained beds than pinks or border carnations, which would be killed by water-logging in winter.

Pollution resistance. Carnations and pinks have a far greater resistance than most plants to smoke pollution of the air, and are thus of great value in or near industrial centres. Such failures as do occur seem to be due to the fact that the soil in such areas quickly becomes acid, but this is easily countered as explained later.

Carnations and pinks are also highly resistant to salt spray. In some seaside places where this trouble occurs from time to time, they are usually among the few kinds of plants which are unaffected.

Light. As has been said, one of the most important requirements is plenty of light, and the sunniest position is the best. If the sun shines on a bed for only part of the day, it is usually fairly satis-factory provided there is plenty of light from the sky, but if there are overhanging trees trouble can be expected.

Air. A free circulation of air is important, and although draughty places should be avoided, the plants prefer wind to shelter. Large bushes, or anything that makes the air stagnant, can lead to trouble.

Air is particularly important at the base of the stem, and any leaves or other matter which may collect there should be removed. Organic mulches should *never* be used.

In extremely exposed places windbreaks do no harm, provided they do not shade the site, but they are not necessary. In proof of this, excellent hardy dianthus may be seen growing near cliff edges on the north coast of Kent, without the slightest shelter from the bitter north-east winds in winter.

Generally speaking, the outdoor kinds do best in the highest part of the garden, but this is not usually the best place for a greenhouse. In the first place, the ventilators are likely to form channels in which draughts are produced, and secondly, if the greenhouse is heated the loss of heat is excessive in a windy position.

In any case, since watering is under control in a greenhouse, far less movement of air is needed to avoid excessive moisture than is the case outdoors. Some shelter from wind is therefore desirable in the site for a greenhouse, though it should not be in a pocket of stagnant air.

Drainage. It is surprising how many gardens are badly drained without their owners' being aware of it. This may be due to the fact that the water-level becomes high only in the winter, when the perennial plants are dormant, and many perennials will stand a certain amount of waterlogging when dormant. Many other plants will not stand excess wet at the roots, and carnations and pinks are among them. It thus often happens that they survive their first winter quite successfully, because then the roots do not go down more than a few inches. During the following summer, the roots grow down to about a foot or so, and when the water-level rises in the winter, the bottom parts of the roots are submerged.

This causes a rot which creeps up the roots, until at the end of the winter the roots have almost entirely rotted away. During the cold weather, the plant does not need much water, and there is no sign that anything is wrong. When the ground dries in spring, and the weather gets warmer, the rotted roots cannot supply enough moisture, and the plant shrivels up and quickly dies.

If there is a doubt about the drainage, a simple test is to dig a hole about 18 inches deep and observe it through the winter. If water collects in the hole, its behaviour should be noted. If the water remains only for an hour or two, or even for a day or two after very heavy rain, there is no need for special precautions. If, on the other hand, water stays in the hole for long periods at a level higher than 12 to 15 inches from the surface, action must be taken.

Many books on general gardening deal with how to drain gardens, but, before embarking on any scheme, it is necessary to consider where the drainage water can go. Probably in most small gardens there is no outlet for the water which can be used without causing damage to someone. Drainage to a sump is usually unsatisfactory for dealing with winter drainage, because in winter the sump is likely to fill of its own accord.

Raised beds. Usually the easiest solution to the problem is not to take the water away from the plant, but to take the plant away from the water. This is done by making raised beds. Since it is necessary only to keep the surface of the soil 15 inches or so above the standing water-level, it often happens that raising a bed a mere 6 inches or so will make all the difference between success and failure.

Any desired method of supporting the soil in the raised bed may be used. An informal wall made of old bricks goes well with pinks and carnations. Whatever is used, it should be firm and not likely to give way at an awkward moment. If the bed is next to the lawn, it should be remembered that it is difficult to cut grass close to a vertical surface. This difficulty can be overcome by putting a flat surface, say of concrete, a few inches wide at the bottom of the wall slightly below the level of the grass, so that the side of the mower can run over it without the blades touching the concrete, or the side of the mower scraping the wall.

The soil at the top of the bed must, of course, be topsoil, and not soil from lower down, called subsoil. Naturally it should be mixed into any existing topsoil there may be, so as not to form layers, but forking over after adding the new soil should take care of this.

SOIL

Although a vast amount of experimental work has been done on it, soil is such a complex material that there is an enormous amount which we do not know about it. Thus it often happens that what works in one place does not work in another, and treatment given to test some theory or other, works, or does not work, for quite a different reason to the theory which the experimenter thinks he is testing. One, therefore, has to be extremely careful in applying to one's own garden the results of an experiment conducted elsewhere. This often applies even to results published by reputable scientists, but, unfortunately, self-appointed soil experts abound, and their theories should be treated with even more reserve.

Moreover, there are sometimes secondary effects. For example, a treatment which is quite successful in a laboratory experiment might, in the open ground, cause a dangerous disease organism to flourish.

The beginner, therefore, is well advised to stick to well-tried methods. After experience has been gained, he may, if he wishes, experiment to find what suits his particular garden.

Content of soil. Soil should not be thought of as an inert mass, for it teems with living organisms, some helpful and some harmful. It is better to think of it as living matter which must be kept healthy if the plants in it are to flourish, but, of course, it also has mechanical properties, and acts as a reservoir of chemical substances on which the plant feeds.

Soil can vary from heavy clay, which becomes an unworkable sticky mass in wet weather, to almost pure sand, which goes to a powder in dry weather. For carnations and pinks, about halfway between these extremes is the ideal soil which has enough sand to keep it workable even when fairly wet, and enough clay to hold it together when dry. It would be possible, but usually expensive, to import clay and put it on sandy soil, and *vice versa*, so as to bring it to the ideal condition, but, fortunately, there are cheaper ways of getting most soils into good enough condition to grow exhibition carnations and pinks. In fact, provided drainage is good and liming is attended to, they will grow in any ordinary garden soil, though, naturally, most people will try to get their soil into as good condition as possible.

Bulky organic material. The old-fashioned way of improving both heavy and light soils was to dig in quantities of farmyard manure, strawy horse manure for heavy soils, and cow and pig manure for light. If they are available in sufficient quantity, there is nothing to beat them, but usually they are not, and a very good substitute is the material from the compost heap. No garden refuse should be wasted. A composting expert will succeed in rotting down almost anything organic, and destroy disease organisms in the process, but the ordinary gardener often prefers to rot down only soft and disease-free material. The rest should be burned and the ashes carefully saved for use as explained later.

When improving an existing bed, the compost heap material should be buried to such a depth that it does not come into contact with the roots of newly planted stock.

The only soils which do not benefit from bulky organic material are old garden soil which has been heavily manured for many years, and soil composed of river silt. Sometimes these can be improved by bringing up some of the subsoil and mixing it with the topsoil.

Improving heavy soils. Although adding bulky organic material is about all that can be done to light soils, heavy soils can often be improved by adding ballast or burnt earth. Coal ashes in moderation can do good, but they tend to be acid and too much can do harm.

Lime, which will be dealt with fully later, is a great improver of heavy soils. The best way to apply it is to dig the ground in the autumn and leave it rough in large lumps, sprinkling the lime over the surface. Frost will break up the lumps and allow the lime to mix in. For carnations and pinks, a pound of ground carbonate of lime to the square yard is quite safe, but this amount may release chemicals which are harmful to other plants. If other plants are to be grown, not more than 4 ounces to the square yard should be applied each year.

Naturally, lime must not be applied close to lime-hating plants, such as rhododendrons.

Digging. Deep digging is not needed. Provided the subsoil allows drainage, there is no need to dig through it every year. Sometimes there is a hard rock-like layer in the subsoil, so it is as well to dig into the subsoil once, but it is not necessary to do it again. Normally, therefore, digging over the top spit is all that is needed. The top spit, of course, is that turned over when an ordinary spade or fork is used to its full depth.

Sensible people practise digging so as to make it merely a gentle exercise. The secrets are not to rush at it, not to get too much on the spade or fork at a time, and to use one's weight rather than one's muscles to drive in the tool and make the initial lift of the soil. As each row is opened up, the bulky organic material is put in the bottom of the trench, and covered up when digging the next row. Next time the bed is dug, the organic matter will be mixed into the topsoil, but by then the fierceness will have gone out of it.

Usually there is not nearly as much bulky organic material as one would like, but if there is plenty available it should not be overdone at one time. About a bushel to 2 square yards is the most that should be put on in any year (a box measuring $22 \times 10 \times 10$ inches holds a bushel).

LIME

Lime has already been mentioned as an improver of the mechanical condition of heavy soils, but apart from that it has the important effect of preventing the soil from being acid.

An acid soil is one of the worst things for carnations and pinks. Why this is so is not absolutely clear, for in scientifically controlled conditions they will grow well in soils that are distinctly acid, that is to say, with a degree of acidity which would invite failure outdoors.

pH values. There is a scale used by scientists to measure the degree of acidity of solutions known as the pH (pronounced 'pee-aitch') scale. The term 'pH' has an exact mathematical definition, but a simplified practical explanation is that the pH scale is a scale running roughly from 0 to 14, in which the lower the number the greater the acidity, and the higher the number the greater the alkalinity, with 7 as the neutral point. This is the explanation given in most gardening books, and, unfortunately, much loose talk, based upon it by people who do not understand it fully, is often heard.

Although the scale works very well in the vast majority of gardens, the amateur should remember certain points. Soil is a solid, and solids do not have a pH value, so when we speak of the pH of a soil we really mean the pH of the moisture in contact with the soil. Now most plants grow best when the soil is moderately moist, and not soaking wet, but the pH value of a soil is usually measured when it is soaking wet, and all the simple soil-testing outfits made for amateurs do this. Although the pH reading on a wet soil will almost always give a fair indication of how it will behave when in the right state for growing plants, it does not necessarily follow that it will do so. Furthermore, although the pH value gives the degree of acidity or alkalinity, it is not an infallible indication of the *amount* of acid or alkali present. It is like a thermometer, which tells the temperature of hot water, but does not tell how much water there is; if we wanted to cool the water, we should also have to know whether we were dealing with a teaspoonful or a gallon.

A simple test often advocated is to collect about a tablespoonful of soil from various parts of the bed in a glass, and pour over it about a tablespoonful of spirits of salts (crude hydrochloric acid, a corrosive and dangerous substance). If there is a strong fizzing there is enough lime present. This test could be misleading if the lime is in fairly large pieces, well scattered. For example, one might get the only limestone chip in the whole garden into the sample one was testing! If the lime is finely divided and evenly distributed in the soil, however, the test is a good one.

These warnings have been given because it is so often made out that tests are infallible, which they are not, but, having said this, it should be pointed out that the simple soil testers sold to amateurs are very good indeed, and if used carefully according to instructions, and the readings interpreted according to the charts supplied with them, the odds against a false result are very large.

The above explanation, so far as it goes, of pH, has been given largely because there has been and is so much talk on the subject in relation to many plants. Unfortunately, there is a tendency to apply results obtained in a few experiments, conducted in carefully controlled scientific conditions, indiscriminately, as if they applied to all conditions. Thus some experiments have shown that perpetual-flowering carnations grow best at a pH of 6. There is no harm in following this if the gardener cares to read the original scientific paper (if he can find it), and make sure that all his conditions are the same as in the experiment, but to say that carnations and pinks do best in such acid conditions as this in all soils, is completely contrary to the experience of expert growers over a long period.

Expert experience shows that carnations and pinks are extremely tolerant of lime, growing exceedingly well on soils that contain more chalk than anything else. The only penalty for overdoing liming is the financial one of paying for lime that is not needed.

The practical result of this is that a soil tester should be regarded chiefly as a money and effort saver. A cheap one is all that is needed, and liming will be necessary unless the tester shows that the soil has a pH of 6.5 to 7 or above, or a good fizz is obtained in the hydrochloric acid test on several samples of soil.

It is not always absolutely clear on a cheap soil tester whether the soil pH is 6.5 or 7, but if there is any suspicion that it is below 6.5 lime should be applied. If the tester does not give pH values, pH 6.5 is the value at which most garden plants do best, and this is referred to in the instructions for using the tester.

In conclusion, it is well to remember that carnations and pinks have been well grown for hundreds of years before soil tests were invented, simply by adding lime if in any doubt.

Type of lime. Quicklime can be dismissed at once as a nasty dangerous substance for amateur use, and this leaves hydrated lime and carbonate of lime. Hydrated lime is popular, and if the gardener is used to it, it has the advantage that its neutralising value per pound is greater than ground carbonate of lime in the ratio of 7 to 5. However, its price is higher than ground carbonate, and the carbonate has the advantage that it can be applied at any time, even as a side dressing while the plants are growing. Beginners, therefore, are advised to use the carbonate, either as ground chalk or ground limestone. It is usually sold by sundriesmen merely as 'carbonate of lime'. Contrary to popular belief, it is just as effective on heavy soils as on light.

Lime is lost from the soil in various ways, the most important being washing-out by rain. If the rain falls through polluted air, and absorbs 'smog' acids, this washing-out can be quick. For example, grass does not need much lime, but good grasslands near industrial centres have been known to become derelict through lack of lime in a mere ten years, and carnations and pinks would fail much sooner than grass. The safe rule is to test at least once a year.

Hydrated lime, if used, should be applied after digging in autumn or winter, and unless it rains heavily at once it should preferably be hosed in. If left on the surface for a day or two it clots and is then difficult to wash in. Lime works downwards, and should always be applied to the surface.

If draining and liming have been attended to, it is fairly safe to assume that conditions are favourable for the beneficial organisms that inhabit the soil. If there is bulky organic matter in the soil, whether it is there naturally or has been added as described above, they will have something to feed on and multiply. Land where beneficial organisms are working actively is often said to be 'in good heart'.

PLANT FOODS

Plants do not feed on solid matter; instead, they absorb solutions from the soil. It is quite possible, and sometimes advocated, to grow plants in nothing but an inert medium such as sand, and feed them entirely on solutions of inorganic substances. Some people have had remarkable success with this method when growing pot plants, but it is as well for the beginner to master the ordinary methods first.

It should be understood, of course, that the main part of the solid substance of the plant comes from carbonic acid gas in the air, which the plant absorbs and converts into sugar, starch and wood. The chemicals in the soil, therefore, are really substances which enable the plant to deal with carbonic acid gas (carbon dioxide), its main food. However, since the carbonic acid gas in the air is always there, and does not have to be paid for, many people are inclined to forget it and consider that the soil solutions are the plants' only food. Thus the substances applied to the soil, or present in it, which help the plant to grow, are what are called plant foods.

The nutrition of plants is a vast and complicated subject, which has already been dealt with in a large number of books and treatises. Since the nutrition of carnations and pinks differs in only minor respects from that of most other plants, there is no need to go into the whole subject of plant nutrition, even if space were available to do so. Therefore, it is proposed only to consider the minor differences between carnations and other plants.

Generally speaking, carnations and pinks require much the same foods as other plants, and good growth will result if almost any good compound fertiliser is used, provided, and this is important, that not too much of it is applied. If the nutrients in the soil are increased beyond moderate limits, the balance between the various nutrients becomes important.

The danger that must be avoided is a high level of nitrogen not

Above, A self border carnation *Right,* Border carnations—*Top left:* Heavy-edged picotee. *Top right:* Wire-edged picotee. *Bottom:* Fancies with bizarre markings.

Border carnations.
Top: Self
Centre: Fancy
Bottom: Fancy

Petals with a dark base, paling towards the edge, are not uncommon in perpetual-flowering carnations

Double pinks.
Top row, *left to right*, a fancy, and a bicolor
Bottom row, *left to right*, a self, a bicolor and a self

A laced pink.
Note that anthers are shedding pollen

A single pink with waved petals. Note that in this case also anthers are shedding pollen

An exhibition group of laced pinks

Typical blooms of perpetual-
flowering carnations

Perpetual-flowering carnations
of more informal shape than
those above

Left, Rooted layer of border carnation *Right*, Rooted cuttings of perpetual-flowering carnations

Rooted cuttings of pinks *Left*, a short-jointed, big-leaved variety *Right*, a longer-jointed, small-leaved variety

A group of annual carnation blooms

Part of the Wisley trials of border carnations

Left, Raised bed in large carnation house. Soil cleared before sterilising and refilling. Note ample side ventilators and permanent framework for tying-up wires

Above, The bed shown in left below (from other side) planted and in bloom

Left, Ground bed in large carnation house. Note 3-inch hollow blocks for drainage on natural earth foundation. The earth must be sterilised and covered with sterilised drainage blocks before refilling

properly balanced by potash and phosphorus (these are the three major chemicals required). This can easily occur even if no so-called 'artificial' manures are used. Some plants, such as, for example, roses, can benefit from extremely heavy doses of farm-yard manure, and are popularly called 'gross feeders'. Such plants are happy with large amounts of nitrogen, but carnations and pinks respond with too sappy growth, so even 'natural' fertilisers, such as farmyard manure need care. This is really the same as forcing, which, as has been mentioned, is very bad. If overmanur-ing with nitrogen has taken place, and the plants show a forced appearance, the evil can often be cured by the application of sulphate of potash, say at about 2 ounces to the square yard.

Proportions of major nutrients. This brings us to the subject of 'balance' in fertilisers. The phrase 'balanced' fertiliser is often seen in articles and advertisements, where it is used to mean a fertiliser which has the main nutrients, namely, nitrogen, phos-phorus and potash, in such proportions that healthy plant growth will result from its use.

This leads to two questions, namely, for which plants is it balanced, and what is the effect of nutrients already in the soil? There is really a third question as to whether the nutrients in the soil will be available to the plant, but in the neutral to alkaline soils used for carnations and pinks, all the three nutrients men-tioned will be available to the plants, though as alkalinity increases phosphorus tends to be less available. This is taken into account in the practical advice given later.

The two questions we have to answer are interlocked with each other, for in the soil conditions we are considering, both phos-phorus and potash persist in the soil, whereas nitrogen tends to be lost. Moreover, in heavy and medium soils, the act of liming releases some potash which was previously locked up in the clay particles. Thus if phosphorus and potash remain from previous applications of fertilisers, or potash has been released by liming, it will do no harm to use a fertiliser fairly rich in nitrogen.

On the other hand, a sandy or gravelly soil which was formerly acid, and has only recently been limed, will probably have little or no reserves of phosphate and potash, and in this case a fertiliser too rich in nitrogen can do harm. Thus it could happen that,

C.A.P.—2

according to what was already in the soil, a fertiliser that was highly nitrogenous could do good in one place and could be disastrous in another.

Interpreting experiments. At this point we can draw one definite conclusion, namely, that it is most unwise to generalise from isolated experiences. Thus recommendations from friends who have tried something or other, and found it 'marvellous' for carnations, should be treated with great reserve. It might be good for their soil, but not for yours.

Another warning is to beware of too-wide generalisations from scientific experiments, without proper allowance for local conditions. One example has already been given, namely, that finely ground carbonate is washed into the soil by rain faster than finely ground hydrate of lime, although every chemist knows that in the test tube the hydrate is far more soluble than the carbonate. Another example, directly relevant here, is that scientific experiments seem to show that the requirement of carnations for phosphate is low, and that for potash much higher, whereas practical growers are insistent on high phosphate manuring and often scarcely bother about potash at all. This may well be because, if the soil gets very alkaline, as it may do just after liming, the availability of phosphorus decreases and therefore larger amounts have to be applied.

This may seem very confusing, but fortunately there are two simple practical ways out, depending on whether a small-scale or a large-scale grower is involved. The key for the small man is that high proportions (not quantities) of both phosphorus and potash do no harm, but a high proportion of nitrogen does. Therefore, if he makes sure that his manuring programme provides high proportions of phosphorus and potash, he will be all right. For the average amateur, the cost of doing this is small.

The large-scale grower, however, may find that unnecessary application of manures can run to considerable expense, so it pays him to have an analysis of his soil made by an expert who will advise him what is needed. There was a case recently of a nurseryman who had such an analysis made, and found that, owing to the liberal fertilising of a predecessor, he had enough phosphate in his soil to last twenty years or so.

Trace elements. For the sake of completeness, it is as well to mention the minor and trace elements, which may be required in from small to minute amounts. These have a great deal of publicity nowadays, because sometimes spectacular results follow from the application of minute quantities of an element to certain crops. Much of the publicity also stems from the rarity of cases where deficiency occurs, so that it is news when it does. The ordinary gardener is advised not to tinker with them, for excesses of some of them can be exceedingly harmful. (In fairness it should be said that the sequestrene compounds sold to gardeners are quite safe, but they are not needed for carnations and pinks.) If there are deficiencies of trace or minor elements, it is almost certain that other plants will show symptoms before carnations and pinks, so that anything that affects carnations without affecting other plants is not likely to be a trace element deficiency. Moreover, if one good crop of carnations or pinks is grown, it is proof that the trace element situation is satisfactory.

Contrary to popular belief, liberal applications of so-called 'natural' manures will not necessarily provide trace elements, nor will any system of composting produce an element which is not present in the materials used. If in real doubt about trace elements, the county horticultural adviser should be consulted.

Slow- and quick-acting fertilisers. If we could apply a mixture of fertilisers to the soil before planting which would steadily release the three major nutrients in the correct proportions, beginning with small amounts when the plants were small, and increasing as the plants grew and required more food, everything would be easy. Unfortunately, no such mixture is known. Although some slow-acting fertilisers appear to have a latent period before they release plant food, once they have started, the food released decreases as time goes on. Moreover, the rate at which nutrients are lost from the soil varies. Nitrogen is lost quickly, potash a good deal more slowly, and phosphorus very slowly indeed, particularly in limed soils. Thus not only the amount of plant food decreases, but the balance between the nutrients alters.

The way to overcome the difficulty is to apply slow-acting fertilisers before planting, which will carry the young plants through for a period, and then apply a quick-acting fertiliser to provide the extra food needed as the plants get larger. The nutrient mainly needed as a supplement will be the one most quickly lost, namely nitrogen, and potash in soils which are naturally deficient in it, such as sandy soils.

Most garden plants do not suffer much from a temporary excess of nitrogen, so they will not mind quite a lot of quick-acting nitrogenous fertiliser. As has been pointed out, however, carnations and pinks do not tolerate excess nitrogen, so that great care must be taken not to apply too much. Even so, uneven spreading might cause a local excess near a plant, so the extra precaution is taken of including some balancing nutrients with the nitrogen.

There is one further point. Quick-acting fertilisers are usually highly soluble salts, and a strong solution of any salt will draw water out of plant roots, which may result in what is called 'burning' them. To avoid pockets of strong solution, quick-acting fertilisers should be applied when the soil is moist, and well watered in.

Similarly, quick-acting fertilisers may burn the leaves of plants if they stick to them, so although the soil should be moist, the leaves should be dry, and any fertiliser that lodges on them should be promptly shaken or washed off.

If the basic principles set out above are understood, it should be quite easy to see the reasons for the practical recommendations which follow. It should be pointed out that the treatment advocated is intended to be safe, and should give first-class results without making any soil analysis. This means that it could be wasteful in adding nutrients which are not needed, and money might well be saved by a soil analysis if large areas are to be cultivated. The treatment is quite suitable for other plants which tolerate lime, but again it will probably be wasteful in supplying more phosphate and potash than most plants need.

Soil feeding before planting. The simplest and best treatment before planting is to wait a month or so after liming to let the lime get well into the soil, and then hoe into the top 4 inches of soil bonemeal, and bonfire or wood ashes, each at 4 ounces to the square yard, and old soot, which has been kept dry, at the rate of 2 ounces to the square yard. The bonemeal supplies phosphorus and nitrogen in the ratio of about 5 to 1. It has the great advantage that overdoing the application will not do any harm. Bonemeal releases the nitrogen slowly so that it will not get washed out of the soil, and is thus a long-lasting nitrogenous manure. It is also, of course, long-lasting in respect of phosphorus, but this is of no importance in a limed soil, because there all phosphatic manures are long-lasting, even the highly soluble ones. Bonemeal will not burn roots even if it has been hoed into the soil immediately before planting.

Bonfire or wood ashes supply potash, but they also have a particularly beneficial effect on carnations and pinks, which has not been properly explained. If they are not available, sulphate of potash at 1 ounce to the square yard will supply the necessary potash, but it does not have the specially beneficial effect of bonfire or wood ashes.

The action of the soot is also not clearly understood, because on analysis it seems to be merely a very weak slow-acting nitrogenous manure, and it does not seem to have such beneficial effects on most other plants as it does on carnations and pinks. It should be at least three months old, and preferably more.

If cost is very important, there is a cheaper way of supplying phosphate, namely, by the use of basic slag, which also supplies lime. Good basic slag at 6 to 8 ounces to the square yard supplies both the lime and the phosphate needed, but there are points to be watched. With most manures, the fact that the phosphate is technically known as 'insoluble' does not matter, because it dissolves in time, but with basic slag the insoluble portion really is insoluble, and worthless. The kind used should have a percentage of at least 10%, and preferably more, soluble phosphate. Furthermore, basic slag contains no nitrogen and must be supplemented by hoof and horn manure at 1 ounce to the square yard. If too much hoof and horn is applied, the balance is upset, and it is so expensive that an excess will soon eat into any saving of cost. If one thinks it out, the cost of manures is usually so little compared to the cost of the plants, that it seldom pays to take risks, and the more usual liming and bonemeal is best in the end.

There is a special point about applying potash manures. If they are applied after about the end of September, carnations and pinks tend to become brittle in the late autumn and winter, and the stems may easily snap. Therefore, if the pre-planting fertilising is done after that date, it is best to omit the wood or bonfire ashes or sulphate of potash then, and apply as a side dressing in spring.

After applying the above pre-planting fertilisers, the ground should be left to settle for about a month before planting, watering two or three times if the weather is dry. However, if it is desired to plant before this period has elapsed, it is quite satisfactory to use the method of planting described in the chapter on border carnations (see page 56).

Soil feeding after planting. If the soil has been prepared as described above, a good, quick-acting fertiliser can be made by mixing 2 parts by weight of superphosphate of lime and 1 part of sulphate of ammonia. With ordinary good grade materials this should contain about 12% soluble phosphoric acid, and about 7% nitrogen. (In passing it should be noted that although sometimes called 'acid phosphate', superphosphate does not in fact make the soil acid, whereas sulphate of ammonia does have this tendency.) The above mixture, which should not be kept more than a week or two after mixing, should be applied at 2 ounces to the square yard wherever the use of a quick-acting fertiliser is recommended in the following pages, except where some other rate of application is specified.

If the bed has had the before-planting manuring in late autumn, and the potash manure has been omitted for the reasons stated above, and is to be applied in the spring following planting, sulphate of potash can be applied at the same time as the quick-acting fertiliser. If the potash is to be supplied in the form of wood or bonfire ashes, however, it should not be mixed with the quick-acting fertiliser, but applied about a week beforehand and well watered in.

Treatment of plants in unprepared soil. It may be that, for some reason or other, the correct preparation of the soil before planting has not been carried out, and the plants are already established in unprepared soil. If there is any suspicion that the soil may be acid, or a soil test shows it to be so, carbonate of lime at 2 ounces to the square yard should be given as a side dressing. This may not be enough to neutralise the acidity completely, but it will not harm the plants, and a further test may be made in three to four weeks' time. If wood or bonfire ashes are available, they should be given as a side dressing at 4 ounces to the square yard, and may be mixed with the lime if that is used.

This dressing should be lightly scratched into the surface of the soil, and well watered in. It is not really good practice to apply bonemeal to established plants, though many people do so. The trouble is that if it is left near the surface it encourages the growth of moss and algae, and hoeing it in deeply will almost certainly damage the roots of the plants.

It is better to give two or three applications of the quick-acting fertiliser during the growing season at intervals of six weeks or so. If no wood or bonfire ashes were put on, the first application of quick-acting fertiliser should be supplemented with sulphate of potash at 1 ounce to the square yard.

Proprietary fertilisers. Provided that the initial preparation of the soil has been done as directed, or there is otherwise plenty of phosphate and potash in the soil, most proprietary mixed fertilisers will give good results, provided they are not overdone. If there is not a reserve of phosphate and potash in the soil, those with a high proportion of nitrogen may cause forced growth and resultant damage.

With all quick-acting fertilisers, 'a little and often' is a good motto, and if in doubt it is best to apply too little rather than too much.

Chapter Three

Greenhouses, Indoor Soil, Potting and Watering

Even if the reader has no greenhouse, and no thoughts of getting one, it is recommended that he should read this chapter, because it is hoped that it will further his understanding of carnations and pinks. If no greenhouse is available, there is, of course, still considerable scope. Pinks can almost always be grown to exhibition standards with no greenhouse, and so can some border carnations. Annual carnations can be bought as seedlings already grown and hardened off for planting outdoors, but without a greenhouse perpetual-flowering carnations are not recommended in this country.

If the reader has a greenhouse, he will want to know how far he can use it as it is, and whether it can be modified to make it more suitable. If he is thinking of getting one, he will want to know what kind to get within the limits of the funds available. The ideal house is, naturally, more expensive than those of lower standard, but practically any greenhouse can be used to advantage if its limitations are realised.

The simplest way to answer all the questions at once is to begin with the ideal house, and work downwards through the cheaper structures, explaining their limitations and possible modifications.

Properties of a greenhouse. In essentials, a greenhouse is a device with three purposes, namely, to modify the temperature of the air round the plants, to control moisture, and to control light. Except in the brightest weather, when shading may be needed to prevent scorching of the blooms, carnations need all the light they can get, so reduction of light must be avoided and we shall not consider it here.

To bloom in the winter months, perpetual-flowering carnations need a temperature above a certain minimum, so the greenhouse is useful both for raising the temperature and controlling moisture.

40

Except when a little forcing is permitted to time blooms for a show, border carnations and pinks do not tolerate a high temperature, so the only function of a greenhouse in their case is to control moisture.

One way of raising air temperature is by artificial heat, but, of course, a greenhouse, whether we wish it to or not, automatically traps sun heat. The reason it does this is because glass is transparent to the shorter wavelengths of radiation emitted by the sun, but much more opaque to the longer wavelengths emitted by warm bodies on the earth. Glass is transparent to the visible spectrum, and for some distance into the ultra-violet and infra-red rays on each side of it. This radiation is absorbed into the contents of the greenhouse, and warms it. The contents of the greenhouse become warm from absorbing this radiation, but when they in their turn radiate, they do so on a longer wavelength, to which the glass is not nearly so transparent, so that the heat is kept in and the temperature rises. There is, however, still a certain amount of heat loss through the glass, in fact, about twice as much as through a wall of single-brick thickness. All daylight, even in dull winter weather, has some effect in raising the temperature.

This explanation is given because it has an important bearing on the size of the house. The amount of heat trapped by (and lost through) the glass is proportional to its area, whereas the temperature inside is proportional to the volume of the contents. To take a simplified example, suppose we had a cubic greenhouse measuring $1 \times 1 \times 1$ yard. The five faces of the cube exposed to the light would have an area of 5 square yards, and the volume of air in it would be 1 cubic yard, a ratio of 5 to 1. If now we double the dimensions of the house, each of the five faces of the cube would have an area of 4 square yards, namely, a total of 20 square yards, but the volume would be $2 \times 2 \times 2 = 8$ cubic yards, a ratio of $2\frac{1}{2}$ to 1.

That is to say, for a house of a given shape, the larger it is the more slowly will it heat up and cool down. In actual practice, the shape of greenhouses does not remain the same as they get larger, so matters are evened out a bit. However, very small houses do tend to fluctuate violently in temperature, so the larger house is much easier to manage, and generally speaking the gardener would do well to have the largest house he can afford, bearing in mind that the larger it is the more he will have to pay for fuel if

C.A.P.—2*

it is heated. Nevertheless, although the fuel will cost more, he will get more value from it, since the heat loss from a large house is less *in proportion to its contents* than that from a smaller house for the reasons given.

Choice of a greenhouse. It must be remembered that carnations require more ventilation than most plants. The ideal, therefore, is to get a large house with plenty of controlled ventilation, which either has a heating system or can easily be fitted with one. Such a house could be used without heat for border carnations, or for bloom from perpetual-flowering carnations in the warmer months. With heat it can be used for getting bloom from perpetual-flowering carnations in winter. It is unlikely the gardener will tire of carnations altogether, but if he does his house could be used as a cold or heated greenhouse for other plants, keeping some of the ventilators closed if the plants do not need so much ventilation.

The best type is the span roof greenhouse, and although I have seen magnificent exhibition perpetual-flowering carnation blooms from a grower who has only one 8 × 6 foot and one 6 × 4 foot house, this grower is something of a genius, and the minimum size recommended to the beginner is 12 × 8 feet. It must be remembered that perpetual-flowering carnations can be 4 to 5 feet tall, and allowance must be made for the height of the pots, so there should be a height of 6 feet, from the staging to the lowest point of the roof, that is to say, the eaves. The staging need only be a foot or so from the ground, and since the pots require no light, the greenhouse may be set on brick walls which come roughly to the height of the top of the pots. Border carnations have a maximum height of about 3 feet, so a lower house will do for them.

There should be at least one good-sized ventilator on each side of the ridge, and they should not be opposite to each other or a draught may be set up. There should be at least one large ventilator on each side of the house. This is the minimum. In long houses the ventilators should extend, if possible, all along the side.

The best type of side ventilator is that which is pivoted about one third of the way down from the top, as this promotes the most even flow of air round the plants.

Many ready-made greenhouses do not have the somewhat large amount of ventilation required by carnations, and if one of these has already been purchased, one should try to modify it if possible. The really important point is to have roof ventilators on each side of the span.

A very convenient method of ventilation is by an electric extractor fan fitted at the top of the greenhouse. This can be controlled by a thermostat so as to operate automatically if the temperature rises too much, and saves a great deal of attention. When we consider heating, mention will be made of a heater which blows warm air by means of a fan, and this type can be arranged so that the fan operates whether the heating is on or not. If there is a circulation of air within the house driven by a fan, it will be found in practice that what ventilators there are, act more efficiently, so they can be rather less in area.

A great boon to the amateur who has to leave his greenhouse during the day is the mechanical automatic ventilator. When the heat increases it causes a fluid to expand in a special container, and this operates a system of rods which open the ventilator. Once installed, there are no running costs.

If the gardener can afford only a house smaller than 12 × 8 feet, he will find it rather difficult to get good bloom on perpetual-flowering carnations in winter, but it is possible to grow perpetual-flowering carnations for summer flowering without heat. A large amount of controlled ventilation will, however, be needed.

If border carnations only are to be grown, however, a much cheaper type of structure will suffice. Since they require no protection from the cold, and the house is merely to control moisture, it only has to have enough glass at the sides to prevent rain getting on the plants, and the more open it is the better. Such a house, however, would not be much use for growing most other plants.

Finally, we come to the kind of house that is probably owned by the great majority of amateurs, namely, a small ready-made greenhouse that is already occupied by other plants which it is not desired to discard. Furthermore, the owner does not want to spend money on altering it until he has tried carnations to see if he likes growing them. The grower in this case can grow border carnations in pots in a well-ventilated cold frame during the winter, outdoors in the spring, and bring the plants into the greenhouse when the buds begin to show colour. This has the very great advantage that the opening blooms are not spoiled by rain, and exhibition blooms can often be obtained in this way. Moreover, the house is used in the summer when it is least needed for other plants. This is in fact the way that most people begin to grow carnations under glass.

Heating the greenhouse. Since border carnations and pinks require no heating, and annual carnation seeds can be raised in any greenhouse suitable for raising bedding plants, what is to be said about heating really refers to perpetual-flowering carnations only.

The most practical forms of heating are hot-water pipes heated by a boiler outside the greenhouse, or electricity in some form.

The boiler and hot-water pipes are more expensive to install and cheaper to run. Professional growers favour this system, fired by solid or oil fuel, because of its cheap running costs and its freedom from power cuts. Oil fuel is more expensive to install than solid fuel, but it is easier to control and less costly in labour. It is not often used by amateurs. However, boiler heating requires a considerable amount of attention to ensure that the water gets neither too hot nor too cold. In a commercial establishment, the staff can look after it while attending to their other duties, but the single-handed grower should remember that he cannot take a weekend away from this greenhouse while heating is needed, and an attack of influenza might spoil his season's work. Nevertheless, if there is someone who can be trusted to look after solid fuel heating if he cannot do so himself, this difficulty can be overcome.

Electricity is much less expensive to install, and although the cost per unit amount of heat is higher than with solid fuel, all the heat is produced in the right place, namely, inside the greenhouse. Moreover, with an efficient thermostat, no more heat need be produced than is necessary, and you only pay for what you use. The thermostat also obviates the need for constant attention. Danger from power cuts is far less than one might imagine, because even if they occur they are most unlikely to be of long enough duration to do any harm. Electricity is also clean and the risk of fumes is absent.

Incidentally, it is possible to control automatically by electricity, not only heat and ventilation, but also shading and watering, so an entirely automatic greenhouse is quite possible, but it is not cheap.

Everyone must make his own choice, and, therefore, both

systems of heating will be discussed, but it is not surprising that more and more amateurs are choosing electricity.

The design of hot-water pipes and boiler for a given greenhouse is a matter for the expert, but the following points should be remembered. The usual greenhouse has the flow (or hot) pipes 3 feet or so from the ground, and the staging comes above them. The return (or cool) pipes are usually around 6 to 9 inches from the ground. This system can be used, but it tends to make the air too hot near the lower parts of the plants. It is much better to have the flow pipes near the eaves, as this gives more even heating. Most carnation experts favour 3-inch pipes if the circulation of the water is not assisted by a pump, since they are not so small that they have to be kept too hot, and they are not so large as to take a long time to warm up.

A system which is finding more and more favour with large houses is to use a greater length of pipe of a much smaller bore, namely $1\frac{1}{4}$ inches, and drive the water round them by means of a pump. Much less water is needed in the system, and, therefore, it does not take so long to heat. Moreover, since the water is driven round, the effect of turning up the boiler is felt much more quickly.

Whatever system is used, it should be capable of maintaining a winter night temperature of 7° C. (45° F.).

It is unusual for the outside temperature in Britain to remain much below −6.5° C. (20° F.) for any length of time, so systems are usually designed to provide a temperature of 7° C. (45° F.) inside the house when the outside temperature is −6.5° C. (20° F.). If it should be colder than −6.5° C. for a time, frost protection will be given and the plants will not be harmed.

As has been said, the design of a hot-water system to give this range of heating is a matter for the expert, but calculation is much easier for electricity. The heating capacity of all electrical heaters is measured in watts, whatever their design. All that has to be done is to find out the maximum number of watts that may be required in a particular greenhouse, which is called the 'loading', and get a heating system big enough to supply it.

People are so used to the idea that a motor car with a large engine uses more fuel than one with a small engine (even though this idea is not strictly true if the weight of the car is considered), that they are apt to think that a large heater in a greenhouse will use more current than a small one. With thermostat control, this is not true at all. Keeping a greenhouse at a certain temperature against a certain outside temperature takes exactly the same current whatever the size of the heater, but too small a heater fimply will not cope if the outside temperature is too low. Theresore, one should always have a heater with sufficient loading, and getting one that is larger than necessary costs more to buy but no more to run in normal use.

It is a simple matter to find the loading for any greenhouse. Find the total area of the glass in square feet, including doors, sashes, and metal or asbestos-sheet walls, as glass. Add to this *half* the area of any wood or brick walls. Call this the equivalent area.

Multiply the equivalent area by the difference between the temperature to be maintained and the lowest temperature outside to be guarded against in degrees Fahrenheit. In our case this is $45 - 20 = 25$. Then multiply by 0.37 (or multiply by 37 and divide by 100).

We can simplify this calculation in another way. If we take the equivalent area in square feet, and multiply it by 10, we get the loading in watts of a heater which will maintain a temperature of 7° C. (45° F.) inside the greenhouse when the outside temperature is −7.5° C. (18° F.). If there is no heater of this loading, we get the next nearest one which has a *larger* loading. The local electricity board will always supply information about greenhouse heating, and should have a booklet on the subject available.

There are many forms of electrical heating, for example, tubular heaters and heating cables. Convector heaters do not distribute heat evenly, but many people use them. The fan heater, which blows air over a heating element, has a great advantage for carnations, for the fan can be operated independently of the heating and keeps the air moving at all times, which greatly assists even ventilation, especially if the ventilators are not all that could be desired. Moreover, the installation cost of a fan heater is low.

The thermostat should be of the 24-inch rod type—a less efficient type is very expensive in wasted fuel in the long run, and does not give the best growing conditions.

A thermostat may, of course, be set to different temperatures, but with higher temperatures the cost is more. A rough guide is that setting at 10° C. (50° F.) uses twice as much electricity as setting at 7° C. (45° F.), and setting at 13° C. (55° F.) doubles the consumption again.

It is not wise to rely too implicitly on the markings on the thermostat, and a good thermometer should be put in various places near the plants, altering the setting of the thermostat if necessary.

There is one most important warning. The electrical installation *must* be carried out by a competent electrician, and everything must be waterproof. All appliances must be designed for greenhouse use. Neglect of this could cause a fatal accident, though properly installed electricity is perfectly safe.

Some enthusiasts manage to grow good perpetual-flowering carnations in houses that are really too small for them, using paraffin heaters inside the house. If this is done, the greatest care must be taken to avoid fumes by keeping the wick and the burner unit very clean.

Site of the greenhouse. It has already been pointed out that the greenhouse should not be in a windy place if it can be avoided. The great requirement is light, particularly for perpetual-flowering carnations, since they grow in the winter. For them there should be no interference with light from all sides. If it can be arranged, it is best for the long dimension of the house to run from east to west.

SOIL FOR USE INDOORS

There are two entirely different types of potting composts used nowadays for growing carnations. The first is what might be called the traditional compost, and the second comprises the John Innes potting composts. Each has its advocates, and if each is intelligently used there seems to be little difference in the results obtained. However, it seems that the majority of successful exhibitors at present favour the traditional compost, though there appears to be a gradual trend in favour of the John Innes composts.

The traditional compost. It is probable that the traditional compost allows for a wider margin of error with regard to watering and other cultural matters than other composts. Its disadvantages are that it is troublesome to prepare, the components are often difficult to get nowadays, and it may contain pests and diseases.

On checking the older authorities, the composition of the traditional compost seems to be very variable, and a different recipe is usually given for the first and second potting. Much of the variation is only apparent, and is due to the way in which the proportions are given, such as so many parts of this, $\frac{1}{8}$ part of that, and so many potfuls of something to the barrow load. On breaking down these recipes to percentages of the total volume, however, it will be found that they do not vary much, and the variation between mixtures advocated by different authors is no greater than variation between the recipes given by the same author in different publications.

A good standard recipe is as follows, all parts being by volume: 16 parts turf loam, 4 parts old manure, 2 parts sharp sand, 1 part wood or bonfire ashes, 1 part limestone chippings.

For first potting, the mixture is put through a $\frac{1}{4}$-inch mesh sieve.

For second potting, the mixture is not sieved but chopped up finely with a spade, and a 5-inch potful of bonemeal added to every bushel (a box 22 × 10 × 10 inches holds a bushel).

Turf loam is prepared by stacking meadow turf upside down for six months or so. The old way was then to spread it out and allow chickens to peck over it to remove pests, but the modern way is to incorporate insecticide dust with the soil, following the manufacturer's directions carefully. Chickens or other birds must not, of course, be allowed to peck it over after adding insecticide, for they may be killed by so doing. The soil insecticide favoured until recently aldrin, no longer being available, BHC and DDT are probably the best to use.

The old manure should be stable manure which has been moistened and allowed to ferment under cover, turning the heap over from time to time until it has lost all odour and the straw breaks up readily. On a small scale it is often worth buying ready-rotted manure in bags.

The sand should be sharp, and is to assist drainage. However, with light loams sand is not required, for the mixture should have a moderately heavy texture, too much sand being harmful.

The John Innes composts. The great advantages of the John Innes composts are that they can be bought ready mixed almost any-where, that they are standardised, and that they are free of pests and diseases. They are made to a standard formula published by the John Innes Institute, but there are one or two points to note. The first thing is to make sure that they are obtained from a reputable firm, which takes care in their preparation.

Another point is that they should be used fresh, that is to say *within* two months of making up, in contrast to the traditional compost which should preferably be kept *at least* two months before use.

A vital point which is often overlooked is that the loam must be sterilised. Actually, sterilised is not the right word, for the loam is only partly sterilised. The temperature to which it is heated destroys plant pests and diseases, and this is important, but it also acts selectively on the microscopic organisms in the soil. Thus the beneficial organisms which increase soil fertility are mostly unaffected, whereas the organisms which prey upon them are largely destroyed. Therefore, soil fertility is much higher than in unsterilised soil. If, as is done by some people, the John Innes ingredients are used but without sterilising the loam, quite a good compost results, but it does not have the most important advantages of the formula.

As stated above, instructions for making the John Innes composts are published, but my experience is that the sterilising process is far more tricky than it sounds, and if badly done can result in a mixture poisonous to plants. Beginners are, therefore, advised to purchase ready-made composts.

Precautions. Most growers use the John Innes composts as made up and suffer no trouble. Some growers, however, find that although things go well at first, the compost in time becomes too acid for carnations. This may be due to faulty watering, but to be quite sure it does no harm to add a 5-inch potful of limestone chippings to each bushel of compost, which will prevent its becoming acid later.

Cleanliness is essential when using these composts, for they will be spoilt if unsterilised soil gets into them. Those who do not use clean tools, pots and benches are like a surgeon who carefully sterilises his implements and then throws them on a dirty floor before use.

There are different grades of John Innes potting composts. For first potting use No. 1, and for second potting No. 2.

Liquid manures. When plants in pots require extra feeding, the John Innes liquid feed can be given to those in John Innes composts. A good liquid manure for all pot plants consists of $\frac{1}{4}$ ounce commercial potassium nitrate and $\frac{1}{4}$ ounce crystalline dibasic sodium phosphate (also called disodium hydrogen phosphate or *sodii phosphas*) in 1 gallon of water. A good idea is to make a stock solution of 1 pound of each of these substances in $1\frac{1}{2}$ gallons of water, and dilute 1 fluid ounce with 1 quart of water for use.

Assuming there is plenty of phosphorus in the soil, as there will be if the traditional compost is used, a good liquid feed can be made simply by dissolving a heaped kitchen teaspoon (two medicinal teaspoons) of Chilean potash nitrate in 1 gallon of water. This is a variable substance, but works very well.

Both these liquid feeds can de described as 'weak' liquid manures, but if proprietary liquid manures are used it is safer to apply at half the recommended strength, as they are apt to be rather nitrogenous.

POTTING

Large growers usually grow perpetual-flowering carnations in beds in the greenhouse, but this will be dealt with in the chapter devoted to those plants. What follows in this chapter applies to potting generally, whether the plants are perpetual-flowering carnations, border carnations, or even pinks, which are seldom grown in pots unless they are intended for exhibition.

The art of potting. Beginners are sometimes puzzled as to why a succession of pots are used when growing plants, instead of putting them straight away into the flowering-size pot. The reason is that with artificial watering, soil in a pot which is not filled with roots goes sour. Therefore, if we put a small plant into a large pot, the soil at the outside tends to go sour before the roots grow into it. However, if the plant is kept too long in the small pot, the roots wind round and round the inside of the pot and form a mat which checks growth. It is then said to be root-bound or potbound. Therefore, we must pot on into a larger size before this happens. Potting on of all plants is, therefore, done when the roots are well through to the sides of the small pot.

The soil water must not remain stagnant in the pot, and the

hole at the bottom must not become choked. Normally there should be no pool of water at the top of the pot a couple of minutes after watering. Some plants need a pot half full of crocks, but this is not so with carnations and pinks. One crock at the bottom is usually all that is needed. A good idea is to use a disc of perforated zinc instead of a bit of broken pot, because this

POTTING A BORDER CARNATION

Left: Potting into 3½-inch pot, using fingers as rammers. *Right:* Potting on to 6-inch pot, using pointed stick as rammer. To finish off, reverse stick and use blunt end.

hardly ever chokes up, and forms an almost perfect barrier against worms when the pots stand outdoors or in a frame.

A plant to be potted, whether a carnation or not, must never be in a dry state, or subsequent watering will merely flow round the roots and the soil on them without wetting them. Therefore, the plants should be well watered the day before potting.

The potting compost must never be too dry or too wet. If it is too dry, it is impossible to firm it enough. If it is too wet, it will puddle into a hard mass in which roots will not grow properly.

The moisture is correct when a sample of soil, squeezed in the hand, remains in shape when the hand is opened, but breaks up readily when prodded.

Carnations like firm potting. The wrong way to do it is to pour in all the soil and press it down with the ball of the thumb, for this makes it firm at the top and loose at the bottom. The right way to do it is to pour the soil in a little at a time and prod it down during the process with the point of a stick or rammer. In a 3- or 4-inch pot, the fingers, held vertically, can be used to firm the soil.

A good gardener never uses his thumb when potting. In 6- or 8-inch pots a piece of thick stick or old broom handle can be used as a rammer.

There should always be a space clear at the top of the pot for watering—it is surprising how many beginners forget this. A quarter inch is enough in a 3- or 4-inch pot, and $\frac{1}{2}$ inch in a 6- or 8-inch pot. More will do no harm.

Plastic pots are used by many growers, and they give good results, though they do not have, with carnations and pinks, the marked advantages that they have with many other plants. Plastic pots should not stand together with clay pots, for if they do it is almost certain that either the plastic pots will be overwatered or the clay pots will be underwatered.

Watering after potting. Some plants (for example cacti), are extremely sensitive to watering during potting. The reason is that some roots are inevitably broken when potting, and in wet conditions they may rot before they heal. Carnations are not as sensitive as many plants, but it is as well to delay watering for a couple of days after potting. They must not dry out, of course, but since potting of border carnations and pinks takes place in cold and damp weather, this is not likely. Perpetual-flowering carnations in a heated atmosphere may require spraying over and keeping in the shade.

A potted carnation must never be watered in dribs and drabs, and when it needs water a good supply should be given, and then no more till the plant needs it again. The surface of the soil may dry while there is still plenty of water below, and to find out if the plant needs water, many growers tap the pot with a piece of wood. If the pot gives a ringing sound, sometimes described as a 'clink', the plant needs water, whereas if it gives a dull sound, sometimes described as a 'clunk', it does not need water. Of course, this does not work with a cracked or plastic pot.

The automatic watering systems previously referred to are not in general use among carnation growers, but they could be used for plants in beds in the greenhouse. They depend on the fact that the electrical resistance of soil rises as it dries. Electrodes are inserted in the soil, and when the resistance rises to a predetermined value, the water is turned on.

Chapter Four

Border Carnations

The vast majority of border carnations in the British Isles are grown planted in the open with no protection whatever, often by people who treat them the same as any other hardy perennials, and excellent results are obtained. As has been mentioned, however, some exhibition varieties require more protection from moisture during their lives, and these are grown under glass.

Nevertheless, even the outdoor kinds may have their blooms affected in some seasons by heavy rain as they are developing, so exhibitors usually arrange some protection from the weather from the time the buds show colour.

All this boils down to the fact that there are really four ways of growing border carnations, namely:

(1) Growing outdoor varieties in the open border without any protection, the usual way for non-specialist gardeners.

(2) Growing outdoor varieties in the open border with protection during the flowering period.

(3) Growing outdoor varieties in pots in the open and bringing them under glass during the flowering period.

(4) Growing any variety in pots under glass the whole time, or nearly the whole time.

Before dealing with the two basic methods, namely, planting out or potting, there are a few points which apply to both.

General considerations. It has already been pointed out that it pays to go to a reputable firm for plants. Incidentally, there is a fraud, interesting because it is more than 300 years old, which consists of selling from door to door plants which are magnificently healthy, but which in due course bear extremely inferior flowers. New housing estates suffer particularly from this fraud. Strangely enough, keen exhibitors sometimes grow these plants, known as 'jacks', because the foliage looks so good in vases at shows where foliage is required.

It should be remembered that a reputable nurseryman will

always advise which varieties do best in the open. In some years even the greenhouse kinds do well in the open, but it is best not to take chances. Of course, *any* variety can be grown under glass. If scented varieties are required, the nurseryman should be told.

It is very important that the main stem of a border carnation should never be broken or pinched out. If this is done, the flowering will be spoilt for a year. This is particularly mentioned because many plants, including most modern pinks, and all perpetual-flowering carnations, are stopped to make them bushy, but *border* carnations never.

BORDER CARNATIONS IN THE BORDER

There is some argument as to whether new stock should be planted in the autumn or spring. The advantage of autumn planting is that, provided it can be completed by the end of October, the roots get a hold on the ground before the cold weather comes, and thus can get away to full growth early in the spring. Against it is this, that if there are to be any winter losses, it is better for the nurseryman to bear them than the buyer. However, there is very little in it either way, and plants put in before about the middle of April are usually as good as autumn planted ones, and often even the end of April or the beginning of May is satisfactory.

The best distance apart is 15 inches, and this allows the plants to bloom for two seasons. If it is intended that they should remain in the ground longer than this, the distance should be increased to 18 inches. If space is restricted, and the plants are to bloom for only one season, then the planting distance can be 9 inches, but this is the minimum for good results.

Depth of planting. This is extremely important, for if carnations are planted too deeply they become very susceptible to stem rot. Stem rot chiefly attacks plants in the winter following their first blooming, and, as one would expect from the name, the main stem rots at or just below ground-level. During the winter the plant looks fairly normal, because it does not need much moisture, but as soon as the warmer weather arrives it shrivels up. On lifting the foliage the stem comes away from the roots at about ground-level.

The golden rule is to plant *firmly* but not *deeply*, bury the *roots* but not the *stem*. Actually a little of the stem is buried, but only ¼ inch or so. The base of the lowest pair of leaves must be clear of the ground. Beginners are tempted to plant too deeply in order to make sure that the plant stands upright, but the correct way is to plant as stated, and then keep the plant upright by tying it to a short stick. Ring ties, of the type sold for sweet peas, are very useful.

How to plant. If all the manures and lime, etc., have been well washed in, and if the soil is neither too wet nor too dry, but in a nice crumbly condition, planting is easy. However, most people find that conditions, for one reason or another, are not quite right when they wish to plant. The following technique enables planting to be done at any time. Some ordinary garden soil is sifted through a ¼-inch mesh sieve (the size of an ordinary garden sieve) in dry weather and left in a dry place ready for the planting. Before beginning to plant, it is moistened, if necessary, by sprinkling with water and stirring. The right degree of moisture is like that of potting soil, namely, if the soil is squeezed in the hand, it stays in shape, but readily breaks up again if gently prodded.

Place the container of soil to the left of the planting place, and dig out a hole with the trowel big enough to take the roots and about two handfuls of soil. Pick up a handful of soil with the right hand, and take the stem of the plant in the left hand. Adjust the height of the plant so that the base of the stem will be ¼ inch below soil-level when the hole is filled. Pour the soil from the right hand into the right-hand side of the hole, filling up one side of it, and then grip the stem of the plant with the right hand, and pick up a handful of soil with the left hand.

Now fill up the left-hand side of the hole, and place both hands flat on the soil around the plant, and press firmly.

Finally, put in a short stick and loop a ring tie round the plant and stick.

This procedure takes far longer to describe than to do, and because it is standardised most people get very quick at it, in fact often quicker than they can plant in the ordinary way. If the weather is damp it is best to delay watering in for two or three days, and a flower pot inverted over the plant will conserve moisture. However, the plant must on no account dry out, and if in any doubt it is best to water.

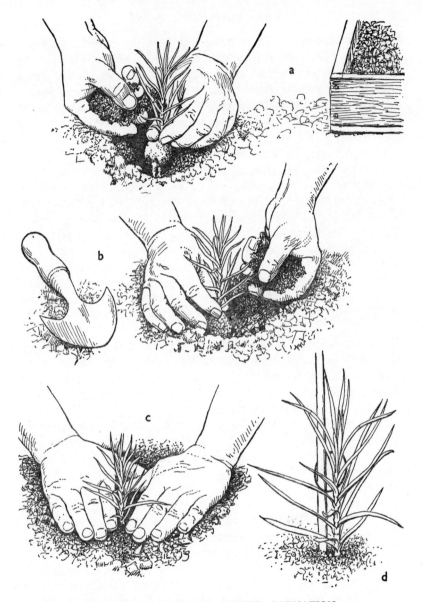

PLANTING A PINK OR BORDER CARNATION

(*a*) Steady plant with left hand, pour soil into right side of hole with right hand. (*b*) Change grip on plant to right hand, pour soil into left side of hole with left hand. (*c*) Press down firmly with both hands. (*d*) Secure to short stake with ring tie.

Winter treatment. If the planting has been done in the autumn, the plants need only a little care during the winter. One should make sure that plants are not snapped off in gales, so the sticks and ring ties should be checked. It is important that dead leaves or other rubbish should not collect round the stems, or stem rot will be encouraged. Rust disease should not appear on young plants, but if it does it should be dealt with as set out later, in the chapter on pests and diseases.

In some districts birds, almost invariably sparrows, will peck out the stems of carnations and pinks. If this occurs the plants must be protected. The use of black cotton is very effective as a scare, but it has been criticised as likely to entangle the birds. Actually this hardly ever happens, and when it does, it is due to the cotton being slack and too close to the ground. Tying to a whippy twig will keep the cotton taut, and if it is kept taut 6 inches above the ground no birds will be entangled. This danger normally occurs from about October to March, though a plant freshly out of the greenhouse may be attacked at any time.

Spring treatment. The application of fertilisers in spring has been dealt with in Chapter 2, and scratching them in will break up the crust on the surface of the soil caused by the winter rains. It is important to break up this crust, but carnations are shallow-rooted plants, and greatly resent disturbance in the main growing season. Any hoeing, therefore, should be more in the nature of surface scratching less than $\frac{1}{2}$ inch deep. This is the reason why a good gardener, who keeps his hoe going regularly and vigorously, is often less successful with carnations than a slack one, who leaves them entirely alone.

It is better to get weeds out when they are small, for getting out big weeds disturbs the soil unduly and may weaken the carnation roots. Short hand tools are best, since a slip of the hoe can break the main stem with fatal results.

It has already been pointed out that mulches of bulky organic matter must never be used, because of the risk of stem rot. Since hoeing must also be restricted, one would expect that watering would be needed. In fact, carnations withstand dry conditions well, and watering is not usually necessary. In very dry weather watering may be needed for best results, and if in doubt water should be given, provided it is applied as a thorough soaking.

Sprinkling the top of the soil can do nothing but harm. Contrary to popular belief, it is not necessary to wait until the sun is off the plants. They can be watered in full sunshine, but, naturally, the water evaporates more quickly in these conditions, so more must be applied.

Mulches of inorganic material, such as limestone chippings, do not harm the plants and may be used, but many people do not find them very effective.

The flowering period. Carnation flowers are heavy, and some support is needed for the stems, which grow 2 to 2½ feet high in most cases, though sometimes 3 feet or a little more. With skill it is possible to push twiggy branches of bushes into the ground so that the stems grow through them and are supported by the twigs, but while this is fairly easy with pinks it is not so easy with carnations. Usually a 3-foot cane is used, and the main stem tied to it with a small loop of string or raffia, or a wire ring tie. The side stems are supported by larger loops of string. There are proprietary carnation supports which provide a circle of wire round the stake and plant, and these are very effective. The lower, non-flowering shoots are not supported.

Disbudding. There is a bud right at the top of the main stem, which is called the crown bud, and this usually provides the largest and best bloom. There are also side stems growing out of the main stem, long at the bottom of the main stem and getting shorter towards the top. Each of these side stems also finishes with a bud at the end.

With plants flowering for the first time, it is a great mistake to disbud too much, as it causes the remaining flowers to be too coarse and often to split their calyxes. A good method is to remove all buds below the crown bud for a distance of 2 or 3 inches, and leave one bud only at the end of each side stem. This should not be done too early, the buds being removed when about ¼ inch in length.

Protection from weather. As has been said, most amateurs do not protect their blooms from the weather, though many exhibitors do, if they grow them in the open. Protection can vary from a simple waxed paper cone wired to the stake, to what is practically a glassless greenhouse put over the plants, the glass being laid on the framework at the danger period. This danger period begins when the petals are partly developed and sticking out beyond the calyx. Rain at this time can cause rough flowers, and rain, later, can mark open flowers.

After flowering, layering is attended to, and this is dealt with later in this chapter.

Older plants. Unlike some members of the genus *Dianthus*, border carnations should not be encouraged to flower a second time in the same season. Such flowering is usually too late in the year for the flowers to open properly, and the plants are ruined for the next year. Therefore, it is best not to stimulate them after flowering with fertilisers or excessive watering. Water should only be given if there is a severe drought.

There is some dispute as to whether old plants should be fed at all in the autumn; some people say it makes them sappy and liable to winter damage. However, it is probably better to give them a small amount of food to build strong roots before the winter sets in. After the autumn rains have begun, say in the second half of September, a side dressing of soot, which must be at least three months old, at about 2 ounces to the square yard, can have most beneficial effects.

Apart from this, the winter treatment of old plants does not differ from that of young ones, except that they are not so likely to break in the wind, and usually no winter staking is needed.

If carnation rust appears, it should be dealt with as set out in the chapter on pests and diseases.

The plants will certainly require some fertiliser in spring as recommended in Chapter 2.

Older plants have a large number of main flower stems, but not usually so many buds on each. Some judgment is required on how many buds to leave, but very often the wisest course is to leave only the bud at the top of the main stem, that is to say, the crown bud. Otherwise treatment during the flowering period is the same as for young plants.

Older plants may be propagated by layers in the same way as young plants, but most exhibitors prefer to get their layers from young plants.

It is possible to leave border carnations in the border for three or even four years, but most keen growers prefer to have them up after the second blooming and replant. There is one treatment that is particularly effective with plants grown from seed, and can also be used for named varieties, and that is to layer a number of the shoots on second-year plants (or all if there is time) and leave them where they are, without severing them from the parent plants.

A few hints. It is sometimes necessary to move an old carnation plant to another site. This can usually be done quite easily in autumn, and there are few failures, but trying to do the same thing in spring almost always leads to trouble.

A sharp frost often loosens and lifts small plants which have recently been put into the open ground. Therefore, after a thaw, any newly planted stock should be inspected, and if necessary firmed in again.

If the same kind of plant is grown too frequently in the same piece of ground, pests and diseases of various kinds are apt to build up to dangerous levels. How long this takes varies according to the kind of plant and local conditions, so no hard and fast rule can be given. If in doubt, and if space will allow, it is best not to grow two successive crops of carnations in the same bed. However, there are cases where carnations or pinks have been grown for ten or fifteen years successively in the same bed without harm, though this should be regarded as rather exceptional.

BORDER CARNATIONS IN POTS

It may seem curious at first that there are many people who grow a hardy plant under glass, but the fact is that by so doing, an amazing degree of perfection can be obtained in the blooms. Indeed there can be few other plants, indoor or outdoor, which can produce the supreme elegance of form and colour of a border carnation bloom grown under glass.

The most important period to have the plants under glass is from the time the buds show colour until the blooms are fully developed. The next most important time is in the late autumn and winter, and it helps to have the plants under glass in spring, though this is less important. Glass also helps while the plants are being layered.

Ventilation. It has been pointed out that the large amount of air required in late autumn and winter makes border carnations unsuitable companions for many other greenhouse plants grown by amateurs, though some plants, such as many alpines, are exceptions. The method of growing outdoor varieties in pots in the open during the winter, and bringing them into the greenhouse for flowering, is not practised by many people. Exhibitors usually grow in the greenhouse throughout the year, planting only their surplus plants in the open border. A good method for beginners, who wish to use their greenhouses for other plants requiring less air in the winter, is to grow in pots in a cold frame during autumn and winter, keeping the light propped open. When the main stems begin to lengthen for flower, usually in March, the lights are removed, the plants being then exposed to the weather until they are brought into a greenhouse when the buds show colour. It should be remembered that for a week or two after removing the lights, the plants are very susceptible to bird attack, so some black cotton should be used.

What follows regarding cultivation applies to plants grown wholly in a greenhouse, but requires only a little adaptation if the plants are grown partly in a frame.

It has been emphasised, and can hardly be emphasised too much, that the great key to success is plenty of air at all times.

Potting. There are two ways of potting border carnations for flowering, and which one is ultimately going to be used must be considered when doing the first potting. They may either be flowered as one plant in a 6-inch pot, or two in an 8-inch pot. The first is probably best for beginners, but the advantage of growing two in an 8-inch pot is that more plants can be accommodated in a given space. The larger pots do not dry out so quickly, so less frequent watering is needed, but on the other hand it is much easier to over-water if the grower is not experienced. There are a few small-growing varieties, mostly picotees, which are flowered singly in a 5-inch pot. For two of these kinds in a pot, the usual 8-inch pot is used.

It is as well to do this as early as possible, so the plants should be obtained as rooted layers in the autumn, say from September onwards. One plant may then be potted into a 3½-inch pot, or two into a 4-inch pot, if they are ultimately going to be grown as a

pair in an 8-inch pot. As with outdoor planting, it is most important not to plant too deeply, and the bases of the lowest leaves
must be clear of the soil. The plants should be kept shaded for a
day or two, then watered and put in full light.

Ventilation is simple, for all the air possible is given, short of
draughts. Watering is not difficult. The soil in the pots must not
remain soaking wet, but it must not get very dry. The roots do
best when the soil is moderately moist, and to secure that, it is
best to wait until the soil is getting fairly dry, and then give a
thorough watering.

With experience it is fairly easy to tell by the look of the plant
whether repotting is needed, but the beginner can look at the
roots. This is done when the soil is not too wet. Two fingers are
placed on each side of the plant at soil-level, the pot is turned
upside down, and the edge given a sharp tap on the side of the
bench. The pot can then be lifted off without disturbing the ball
of soil. When the roots are through to the side of the pot, it is
time to pot on. The earlier this can be done the better, and it
should be before the end of February for the best results.

The method of potting on has been explained, but particular
attention should be paid to getting the earth firm with a rammer,
not putting the plant more deeply than it was before, and leaving
a ½-inch space at the top for watering.

Spring and summer treatment. In March the soil should be loosened
slightly at the surface, and from then on watering should be carefully watched so that the soil does not dry out. Do not water all
the plants at once, only water those that need it.

From April to May greenfly may attack the plants, and they
must be eliminated before they get a hold. Later red spider may
attack. Both these pests should be combatted as set out in the
chapter on pests and diseases.

Staking and disbudding are the same as for plants in the open.

In bright summer weather the house can get too hot, and it is
as well to apply a spray of whitewash to the outside of the house.
Some people use a mixture of clay and water, or proprietary
brands of greenhouse shading. Not much is needed, only a light
spatter to break the fierceness of the sun. Greenhouse blinds on
the outside of the house are, of course, excellent.

The plants should be well watered the day before cutting the blooms, and the best time to cut is early morning or late evening. If the blooms can stand up to their necks in water in a shaded draught-free place for twelve hours before arranging, it improves their lasting qualities. Water should never, however, be allowed to get on the blooms.

Some growers apply liquid manure every fortnight from the time the buds are seen until they begin to show colour, but some do not. The beginner is advised to try it on a few plants the first year, to see if it suits his particular methods of cultivation.

Border carnations are not often grown for a second year in pots. After flowering they should be layered as described below, and any plants not required for this purpose can be planted outdoors for blooming the next year.

PROPAGATION BY LAYERS

The natural propagation of carnations is by seed, which is a sexual process resulting in variation between the individuals produced. This variation is great in the case of border and perpetual-flowering carnations and the cultivated pinks, so plants which are required to be true to the individual from which they come are propagated vegetatively; that is to say, parts of the original plant are induced to root and grown separately. It will be remembered that all the plants so derived from an original seedling are called a clone.

Some plants, such as thistles and perennial poppies, will produce a new individual from a piece of root. Others, such as winter jasmine, root very easily from any part of the stem which is buried, but though some pinks will do this to a limited extent, carnations hardly do so at all.

Carnations and pinks, therefore, have to be propagated in a more fundamental way. If plant tissues are injured, they heal by forming callus, which is scar tissue, and this is so with carnations. Plants vary greatly in the speed with which they will form callus, and in the speed with which roots will grow from it. In some plants the process can be speeded up by the use of chemicals, or rooting hormones as they are called, but carnations are extremely insensitive to them, so little or no benefit results from their use. Another way of speeding up the process is by using a mist propagator, and carnations respond to this.

If a cutting is severed from the plant and inserted in soil to root,

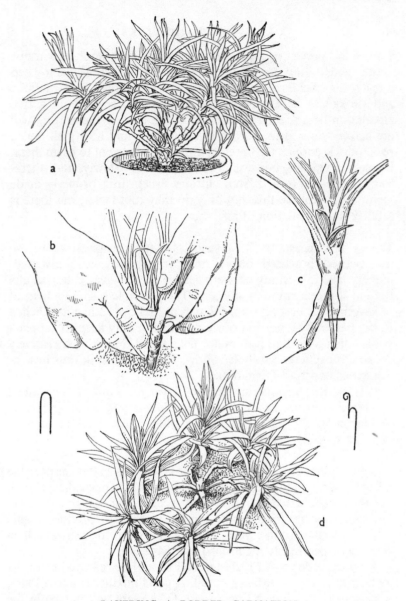

LAYERING A BORDER CARNATION

(*a*) One-year-old plant with lower leaves stripped off ready for layering. (*b*) Cutting stem to make layer. (*c*) The layer after the first cut. The tongue should be trimmed off just below the joint where indicated by line. (*d*) The layers are bent down and pressed into the soil, keeping the cut open, and pegging down with a wire pin shaped as shown in drawing.

it must be prevented from drying up by being kept in a moist atmosphere until it has made roots, and the normal way is to keep it in a frame of glass or polythene. As we know, however, carnations and pinks can be kept only for a limited time without a free circulation of air, so if it takes too long to root the cutting will die before roots form. Perpetual carnations, and nearly all pinks, root quickly enough for the close air in the frame not to harm them. Border carnations, however, root much more slowly, and, therefore, cannot be rooted from cuttings except in a properly made mist propagator. In this, not only do they root faster, but there is a fairly free circulation of air.

Theory of layering. In the absence of a mist propagator, we use the method practised before mist propagators were invented, namely layering. Many growers believe that it gives better results than mist propagation in any case. The principle is simple. Instead of severing the cutting from the parent plant, we leave it attached to the parent by a portion of stem. This not only keeps it supplied with moisture so that it does not have to be kept in an excessively moist atmosphere, but it also allows food to reach it, thus hastening callus and root formation.

It is worth remembering that the layer does not need so much food and moisture as an actively growing shoot, so the part connecting it to the parent plant can suffer quite a lot of damage without spoiling rooting.

Practice of layering. The best time for layering is as soon as possible after flowering, but there is no need to make a frenzied rush at it, for the season extends over several weeks. It is best not to begin before flowering, for layering too early tends to produce plants which flower twice in a year, which is not good for reasons which have been previously mentioned (see page 60).

First of all the top 2 inches of soil should be removed from the pots, and replaced with sandy soil. A good mixture is 1 part loam, 1 part peat and 1 part sharp sand. (The plant will not be in the peat long enough for acid conditions to develop.)

A good layer consists of the top portion of a side stem, leaving about five pairs of developed leaves in addition to the growing point at the top. All the leaves below this are stripped off. As with most plants, callus and roots form most readily at a joint, and, therefore, the cut should finish off just below the joint below the lowest pair of leaves.

Sterilising the knife. Though spread of disease on the propagating knife is less likely than many people think, it is better to be safe than sorry. Most directions in gardening books for freeing the knife of possible diseases are quite useless, but the proper way is very simple. Have a pot or glass of methylated spirit deep enough to immerse the blade in the spirit to its full length. Have also a small lighted spirit lamp. After dealing with each parent plant, wipe the knife on a clean damp cloth if there is any visible dirt on it, dip it in the spirit, and hold the blade horizontally in the flame until the spirit has burnt off. Use the knife on the next plant without further wiping. The whole operation takes about five seconds.

To make the cut, the point of a thin penknife or a special layering knife is pushed into the stem just below the lowest pair of leaves left on the stem, and the cut continued downward through the joint below, splitting the stem in half. The knife is then brought out sideways away from the centre of the parent plant. If it can be brought out neatly just below the joint the cut is finished, but if a tapering tongue is left, it should be cut off just below the joint.

The bottom of the layer is pressed into the soil near the edge of the pot in such a way that the cut remains open, and secured with a layering pin. At this time of year it does not matter if the bases of the lowest leaves are below the surface, remembering that when the layer is subsequently potted they must be above the soil.

The layering pin is merely a piece of wire bent in the shape of a hairpin which is hooked over the stem connecting the layer to the parent plant. It is best made of galvanised wire, and it is an improvement if one side of the wire is bent upwards about an inch of the way down, so that it sticks up above the soil. This makes it easier to pull out after rooting. The long side of the pin should measure about 3 inches.

The pot of layers should be kept watered, and in dry weather frequently sprayed over, for five or six weeks, when the layers will have rooted and can be severed from the parent plant. It is a good idea to leave them for a week after severing before lifting.

After this they may be planted out or potted. The roots should not be left to grow too long before lifting and potting.

Some finer points. Sometimes the stems are too long to bend readily to the side of the pot without snapping at a joint. It is then a good idea to pinch the stem between the joints with fine-nosed pliers, or between the finger-nails if strong enough. Often it is enough to pinch only two or three joints about halfway between the parent plant and the layer.

Do not put down too many layers in the pot. Overcrowding does not pay, and the pot should not have more than shown in the illustration. If in doubt, a shorter layer is better than a long one. Make sure each layer is upright. Get the layer as close as possible to the edge of the pot, for rooting is better there. Be careful the soil does not dry out.

The principles of outdoor layering are exactly the same as layering in pots, except that as more space is available every good shoot can be layered. On the other hand, no more need be put down than are required, and the parent plant can stay where it is for another year.

Usually the whole area round the plant is not covered with rooting medium, but only a mound of it where each layer is to go. The surface of the soil should be stirred before putting on the heap of medium. In stony soil it is sometimes difficult to push in the layering pin, and if pushed too hard it is liable to go with a rush and break the connecting stem. A way out of this is to put a ring of roofing felt round the parent plant about 4 to 6 inches away from it, securing the ends, which should overlap for a couple of inches, with a clip. If this ring is about 2 inches high it can be filled with rooting medium just as if it were the top 2 inches of a pot. This has the advantage that not only does the layering pin go in easily, but also the clip may be removed and the ring opened to see when the layer has enough roots.

Watering may be more or less often than in a greenhouse, depending on the weather. Do not be deceived by light showers which may make the soil look moist on top, when it is in fact dry underneath.

Chapter Five

Pinks

As mentioned in Chapter 1, a fundamental change was begun in pinks about fifty years ago. It took some time for this change to become effective and work through to the ordinary gardener, and it was held up by the Second World War. The result has been that in the space of the past twenty years or so a tremendous change has taken place in pinks and the growing of them.

THE OLD GARDEN PINKS

Those whose memories go back to the twenties of this century and before will remember beds of pinks, usually white in colour, with masses of fragrant blooms in June. The best known of these was Mrs Sinkins, though in many cases plants grown under that name were not the true variety but somewhat similar white pinks. Taken individually, each bloom was a poor ragged thing with a split calyx, but they made up in quantity what they lacked in quality, and, of course, the scent was magnificent. Many of these old pinks began to lose vigour in the thirties, and there were two reasons for this. In the first place, no variety of pink lasts for ever, and the clones began to get old. In the second place, they were propagated by pulling the bushes apart in autumn and planting the pieces. This is a fundamentally bad way of propagation. In the end, it leads to plants which apparently grow well until the buds are just ready to open. At that stage, the poor root system resulting from bad propagation cannot supply enough sap to open the buds, and they rot.

Old pinks still grown. Much as many people consider that the horse and trap had a charm not shared by the motor car, so there are many who like to grow the old pinks. However, it must be remembered that they are old, and will not tolerate the rough and ready propagation that they once did. Those who wish to grow them must propagate by cuttings as described later in this chapter, or by layers as described under border carnations. There

69

are some fairly new pinks still being bred which resemble the old ones in flower and habit, but they are not widely grown, for people who like pinks usually grow either the modern type or the really old varieties.

Habit of old pinks. The habit of the old pinks is almost exactly that of border carnations, namely, a plant which blooms only on the central stem in the first season. The difference between them and the true modern pinks, is that they can be left alone for four or five years before propagation, and if this is to be done a planting distance of 12 inches apart is about right. Old varieties, and newer varieties of the old type, are often called 'garden pinks'. This is apparently left over from the days when exhibition pinks were grown under glass, and although all pinks are now strictly garden plants the name has persisted.

MODERN PINKS

The flowers of the true modern pinks are larger and more regular in shape than those of the old pinks. Some of them are almost perfect rosettes, and there are no split calyxes. There is widespread ignorance of how good they are. In fact, if grown in a front garden, the commonest remark of passers-by is 'What beautiful carnations!'

The chief practical difference between modern and old pinks is in the habit of the former, which is somewhere between that of a border and a perpetual-flowering carnation. After the main flowering in June, the side growths elongate and flower later in the same year. How long they take to do so varies from variety to variety, but there are some which in favourable conditions flower three times in the season, rather after the manner of a hybrid tea rose. Unlike the old pinks, breaking off the main stem does not prevent flowering for a year, and it is the usual practice to stop them, that is to say break off the main stem deliberately. The art of doing this is explained later in the chapter.

It is not surprising that the modern hybrid pink is, among amateurs, the most popular of all dianthus, but the number of people who grow them is far smaller than it should be. Even quite experienced gardeners are sometimes misled by their memories of the old pinks, and it not infrequently happens that they grow carnations for a year or two and then suddenly realise that it was pinks they wanted all the time. In some ways beginners may have an advantage over more experienced gardeners, for they do not have to unlearn so much.

General cultivation. The preparation of the soil, planting and cultivation of pinks is the same as in the case of border carnations outdoors, with one or two important exceptions which are noted later in this chapter. However, in nearly all respects there is a wider margin of error, so that pinks will often thrive in conditions where border carnations would grow badly or die, though this should not be taken to mean that we can be careless.

Planting. As pinks bloom a month earlier than border carnations, they cannot be planted quite so late, but since the roots get hold of the ground quickly, it is safe to plant up to the end of March, and sometimes mid-April is all right. They can be planted in autumn, which exhibitors prefer, or in mild spells in winter. The vital point, as with border carnations, is not to bury the stem. Planting distances for modern-type pinks can vary from 8 inches apart for small-growing varieties which are to remain for only two years, to 18 inches for the stronger kinds, which are to remain for three years. It is usual, however, to grow modern pinks for only two years in the bed, and in that case 12 inches is enough for a strong-growing variety. Twelve inches is also, it will be noted, the planting distance for the old-type pinks, but these can remain for four or even five years since they grow much more slowly. The wider distances give a bare appearance to the bed for the first year, and interplanting temporary plants may be an improvement. Small hardy annuals are suitable, but a really excellent plant is the small or butterfly gladiolus. Gladioli are deep rooting and do not compete with the shallow roots of young pinks, and the foliage does not cast much shade. They have to be lifted in autumn in any case, which leaves the ground clear for the pinks to grow larger.

Apart from stopping, which will be dealt with later, winter and spring treatment is the same as for border carnations.

Removal of flower. Modern pinks often produce small flower buds in late autumn and winter, and although these bloom very early, the blooms are ragged and poor. Any premature flower stems showing developed flower buds in March should, therefore, be removed, which will give the side shoots time to bloom about the normal time.

The only marked difference between the treatment of pinks and that of border carnations up to the time of flowering is that pinks are not disbudded. The only exception is where a small bud is produced so close to the crown bud that there is a danger of the crown bud being pushed sideways. If so, the small bud is removed.

Feeding after flowering. As soon as flowering is over, the old flower stems should be removed, and the plants thoroughly watered. Application of the fertilisers recommended in Chapter 2 helps a great deal. The reason for this is that modern pinks, unlike border carnations, should be encouraged to bloom again in the same season. The old type of pink will not flower again, but the water and fertiliser builds up the plants.

Later care. Varieties which require staking will, of course, have to be staked again for their second and possibly their third flowering. Modern pinks require more water in late summer and autumn than border carnations, because they are actively growing and flowering.

In late autumn a bed of year-old modern pinks will probably contain plants which have flower stems in various stages of development. In the absence of hard frosts these will continue to flower till about Christmas, so they can be left until then. In the New Year stems that have not flowered should be removed, as should also any unduly long and straggling stems.

The treatment for the second spring and summer is the same as for the first. Those modern pinks which, as explained later, have a tendency to flower themselves to death, are particularly liable to do so at the first flowering of the second year, and stopping should be attended to as set out on page 79.

Layering. Owing to the smaller size of the plants, layering is not quite so easy as with border carnations, but it is done in exactly the same way, though it can be begun earlier since the flowering season is earlier. Some of the best exhibitors prefer layers to cuttings, but many people get equally good results from cuttings. The only pink which the beginner is likely to encounter which must be layered is the variety Bridesmaid. A variety which has begun to deteriorate through old age can often be kept going for a few more years by layering instead of taking cuttings.

CUTTINGS

Up to this point differences between the treatment of pinks and that of border carnations have been slight, and any point not specifically covered so far in this chapter may be assumed to be the same for both. When we come to the question of propagation and stopping, however, the differences in treatment are large.

The propagating season begins when flowering is finished, and goes on until the third week in August. Generally, the earlier the better, but owing to the different growth rates of different varieties all plants are not usually ready at the same time. Some people do a few plants at a time as they become ready, but doing one large batch early in July and another early in August usually covers all the plants, and makes the management of the frame easier.

The cold frame used for propagating can be of very simple design. Nurserymen use a cold greenhouse, but in this the cuttings require constant attention by a skilled propagator, so it is not suitable for amateurs. Amateurs require something that provides a moist atmosphere and does not get too hot without constant watching.

An excellent frame for amateurs is a wooden box about 10 to 12 inches deep, with an even top so that a sheet of glass laid on it leaves no gaps. The frame should be placed where it gets full light from the sky, but no sunlight. About an inch of sand (of any kind) is placed in the bottom and thoroughly wetted. Dry sand is not always easy to wet, but a little household detergent in the water helps a lot. After wetting, a dusting of DDT powder inside the frame deters pests, and the glass is put on. The cutting pots are put in the frame as they are done and the glass replaced at once.

Pots and rooting medium. Nurserymen root cuttings in pans, but the ordinary $3\frac{1}{2}$-inch pot is excellent for amateurs, and holds nine to twelve according to their size. It is most important not to overcrowd the cuttings. Nurserymen use pure sharp sand for rooting, but this, of course, contains no nutriment, so the cuttings

must be put into soil at the right moment. A much better plan is
to fill the pot to within 1½ inches of the top with any good soil
or potting compost, and then put a layer of rooting medium on
top, leaving ¼ inch at the top for watering. In this the cuttings
can, if desired, be left without harm for as much as four or five
weeks after they have rooted.

An excellent rooting medium is 3 parts by volume of propagating sand and 1 part of horticultural vermiculite. Propagating
sand is sold by nurserymen, and that known as washed and
crushed river sand is very good, but any sharp clean sand will do.

After filling, the pots are given a good watering, and as soon
as the water has drained away they are ready for the cuttings.

Selecting the plants. The best plants are the only ones from which
it is worth taking cuttings, because taking cuttings from poor
plants is a waste of time and effort. The first requirement is that
they should be healthy and up to the degree of vigour appropriate
to the variety. Since flowers are the object, plants that produce
good blooms freely should be chosen. It is as well to mark them
when in flower, for otherwise there is a tendency to take most
cuttings from those which produce most shoots. This can lead
to a stock which grows freely but flowers poorly.

It is easy to select shoots for cuttings on the old type of pink,
for one merely takes the strongest. Modern pinks which flower
more than once in a season are more difficult, for at propagating
time there are usually three kinds of shoots. The smallest are more
or less dormant; waiting, so to speak, for the others to grow and
flower first. These small shoots tend to remain dormant as cuttings
and are not satisfactory. At the other extreme are shoots which
have begun to lengthen for flower, that is to say the distance
between each joint is increasing. If taken as cuttings, these shoots
rapidly become leggy and hard, and never make good plants. The
correct shoots are in between these extremes, namely strong-
growing shoots which have not begun to lengthen. (If the plants
are to be layered, the same type of shoot should be selected.)

The ease with which unsatisfactory material will root is one of
the chief reasons why stock should be purchased from reliable
firms who know their business.

Making the cuttings. A cutting consists of the growing point with

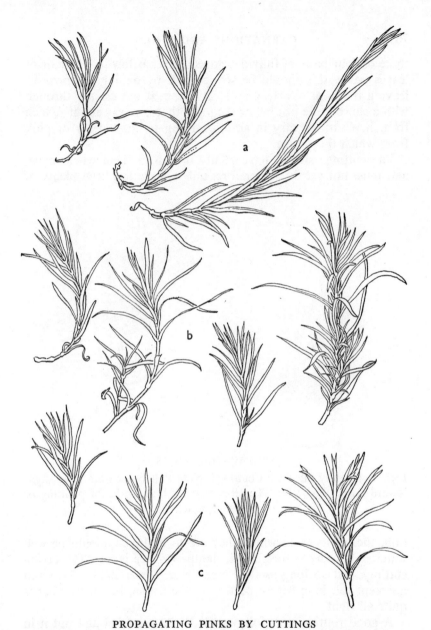

PROPAGATING PINKS BY CUTTINGS

(*a*) Shoots from one variety of repeat-flowering pink. *Left:* Too small and dormant for making a good cutting. *Centre:* Just right. *Right:* Running to bloom and too far advanced. (*b*) Shoots from four different varieties, all suitable for making cuttings. (*c*) Cuttings made from shoots shown in (*b*).

three or four pairs of fully developed leaves below it. The pair of leaves below this should be stripped off by pulling downwards, leaving the joint clearly visible. The stem is cut cleanly through with a sharp knife just below the joint, that is to say about $\frac{1}{32}$ inch from it. Cuttings vary in size according to the variety of pink from which they come.

The cuttings should have plenty of sap in them when made, and must not get dry. Therefore, unless there has been plenty of

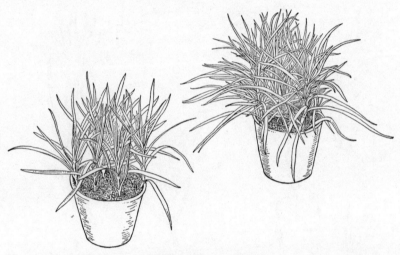

PROPAGATING PINKS

Left: Pot nearly filled with cuttings. Note that outer ones have slight inward slant. *Right:* Pot of well-rooted cuttings ready for planting or potting separately.

rain, the plants from which they are to be taken should be well watered the day before. Dull, damp weather is best for taking cuttings, but so long as they are trimmed in a shady place and not kept too long before putting in the frame, bright weather is quite all right.

A good routine is as follows. (1) Write the label and put it in the pot. (2) Take all the shoots required from one plant. (3) Put them in the shade and syringe them with clean water. (4) Make them into cuttings. (5) Put them in the pot. (6) Sterilise the knife as advised in propagating border carnations. (7) Go to the next plant of the same variety, and repeat as above until the pot is filled. (8) Put it in the frame. (9) Sterilise the knife and begin again.

Inserting in the pot. The cuttings must not be inserted too deeply, and the bases of the lowest leaves must not be buried. This means that they are not very firm in the sand, and it is advisable to give them a slight inward tilt so that they do not fall out when they are watered. As has been said, they must not be overcrowded, and nine to twelve cuttings, according to their size, are enough for a 3½-inch pot.

It is much easier to control the frame if all the cuttings in it are at about the same stage. Since the kind of frame needed is so cheap and easy to prepare, it is as well to use each frame only for cuttings inserted within two or three days of each other.

When each day's batch of cuttings is completed, the pots should be sprinkled with a fine-rosed can to settle the sand round the bases of the cuttings, and the glass put on close. After four or five days the glass should be adjusted to let in a little air, but not enough to let the air get really dry.

After-care. The cuttings root in about three weeks. The beginning of rooting is indicated when the leaves begin to spread out, and the tips of the plants begin to grow. More air is then admitted each day until after about a week the glass is removed entirely. From then on extra care is needed to make sure that the roots do not become dry. The propagating medium on the top of the pots is rather apt to dry out suddenly.

If the pinks are to be potted before planting out, potting into 3½-inch pots can begin as soon as the glass is off the propagating frame. However, it is less trouble to wait a further two or three weeks and plant direct into the ground where they are to flower. If so, they will need watering in dry weather for a few weeks after planting.

It must not be thought that propagation by cuttings is difficult just because the matter has been gone into in such detail. The reason for explaining each step so fully is that it is just as easy and quick to do things correctly as to do them wrongly. Although good results are often obtained by slapdash methods, they sometimes let you down badly.

Some things to avoid. Until quite recently it was thought to be good practice to drop each shoot into a bowl of water as it was severed from the parent plant. The old books even advised soaking the cuttings overnight in water to which a small quantity of potassium nitrate had been added. Hundreds of people did either or both of these with good results, but that was before carnation wilt diseases were so widespread. Pinks are not often attacked by these wilts, but if there are any infected cuttings, the infection can spread through a bowl of water in a matter of minutes.

Two old methods of propagating were by pipings and slips. A piping was made by pulling out the top of a shoot without using a knife. The trouble is that the break usually occurs in too soft a part of the stem, and above instead of just below a joint; both these factors tend to retard rooting. Pipings, however, are better than cuttings taken with a blunt or infected knife.

Slips are complete side shoots detached from the main stem by a downward pull, and may or may not be trimmed before insertion in the sand. The disadvantages are that the main stem is damaged in taking them off, that the base of the cutting is hard and roots slowly, and that the joints are so close together that the bases of several leaves are buried, which may cause rotting.

Pipings and slips still give fairly good results with the old type of pinks, because the upper parts are slow growing and there is plenty of time for the roots to catch up before many flowers are produced. It is a different matter with modern pinks.

There is one fantastic trick which is utterly stupid and never was any good, but is so widespread that it must be mentioned. The base of the cutting was split upward for half an inch or so and kept open with a small pebble—in other words it was like a layer which was not attached to the parent plant. This merely increases the area over which callus must form, and provides a ready entry for diseases. A layer, of course, has to be cut this way, because it is the only way of doing it, but a layer is plentifully supplied with sap from the parent plant which enables it to form callus over a large area. A cutting has no sap from the parent plant to help it, and the smaller the area which must be healed the better. The pebble trick was also done with border carnations, but, of course, is equally silly with them, though, since layering is now the rule, cuttings of border carnations are seldom used.

THEORY OF STOPPING

As has been mentioned, one of the chief characteristics of the modern pink is that it blooms more than once in a season. This means that every stem has a tendency to run up to bloom, and this can lead to trouble with both old and young plants. If the only stem of a young plant runs up to bloom before it has made sufficient growth at the bottom, the plant will be so exhausted by the effort of flowering that it will either die, or take so long to recover that it will never be much good. This is prevented by breaking off the top of the main stem so that side shoots develop before the plant flowers. The trouble with older plants occurs when, for one reason or another, all, or nearly all, the stems run up to bloom at the same time, in which case the plant flowers itself to death. This is prevented by stopping a proportion of them, so that they make side growths to sustain the plant while the remainder flower. At one time there was quite a lot of this flowering to death in the second season, but nowadays varieties which are prone to this trouble usually disappear from the catalogues as being difficult for ordinary gardeners.

The old type of pink should not be stopped as a young plant, or the first flowering period will be missed. Since a modern pink should be stopped, and an old type should not, what do we do if we do not know to which type a particular plant belongs? This difficulty is more theoretical than real. In the case of a modern pink the plant usually solves the problem by lengthening up for flower in the late summer or autumn after it is propagated, and any pink which does this should be stopped. If it has not lengthened up by the following March, and we do not know if it has the modern growth habit or not, we take a look at it. If there seems to be plenty of foliage, either as leaves on the main stem or as side shoots, we leave it alone. If not, we stop it, because even an old-type pink suffers if it flowers without enough foliage, and it is better to lose the first season's flower than the plant.

PRACTICE OF STOPPING

When we stop a pink, it produces 'breaks' or side shoots, and when it has done so it is said to be 'stopped and broken'. The idea is to produce the maximum number of good breaks, and to make a bushy plant that is not too tall. If merely the growing tip is pinched out, only one or two breaks are produced near the

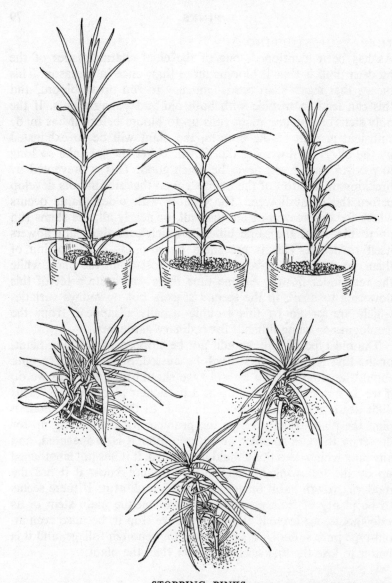

STOPPING PINKS

Above: Three pinks in early autumn. *Left:* Ready for stopping. *Centre:* Stopped at 6th joint. *Right:* Previously stopped and breaking evenly at every joint.

Below: Pinks in bed in early spring. Sufficient side growth so no stopping needed.

top. The proper way to stop is to allow the plant to grow until nine or ten fully developed pairs of leaves have been produced and then snap the stem off at the sixth to eighth joint. The stem snaps most easily in the early morning when the plant is full of moisture. Hold the joint in the thumb and finger of the left hand, and bend the stem above it sharply at right angles with the other hand. Usually it snaps out cleanly, but if not bend it to the opposite side also at right angles. If this fails, do not tug it out, but cut it cleanly as close above the joint as possible.

Modern pinks should be stopped when they have grown to the right stage as described above, but this should not be done so late that the side growths will not develop properly because of cold weather. In the south of England any that have not developed far enough for stopping by about mid-September should be left till the spring before they are stopped. Autumn stopping does not usually delay flowering, early spring stopping delays it for only a week or two, and later spring stopping for a month or more.

Usually pinks do not have to be stopped more than once, but, as has been mentioned, there is the case where all the shoots try to run up to bloom at the same time for the second or subsequent flowering. If such plants seem to have a fair amount of foliage at the base, it is enough to stop about one-third of the stems, which should be broken off about 3 inches from the bottom. If the foliage is sparse, one-half of the stems should be stopped.

No ordinary gardener grows pinks under glass, but some exhibitors do so in order to get blooms unaffected by the weather. In general, the culture is the same as that of border carnations under glass, but there are two important differences. Since propagation begins earlier, and rooting is quicker, the plants are ready for second potting sooner. For best results they should be in the flowering pots by the end of September. The other difference is that they are not kept under glass during the winter, but stand on a bed of ashes outside. They are taken under glass when the buds begin to show colour, and are kept under glass only until blooming is over.

SOME POPULAR ERRORS

Two criticisms aimed at modern pinks are that they are neither so free flowering nor so strongly scented as the old varieties. In fact, the number of blooms on a modern pink in a given period is far greater than on an old-type pink. The confusion has arisen because modern pinks are usually not grown for more than two, or at most three, years before replanting, whereas the old ones went on for four, five or even six years. People are unconsciously comparing a two-year-old modern pink with a five-year-old pink of the old type. If a careful check is made, it will be found that in the first two years from propagation a modern pink will produce at least five times as many flower stems as an old-type pink, and usually more.

The truth about scent is that modern pinks have two distinct scents, one being the old clove scent and the other like that of some perpetual-flowering carnations. The majority of them are not as strongly scented as, for example, Mrs Sinkins, but there are some which have an even stronger clove perfume than any of the old types. If these are required, the nurseryman should be told.

Chapter Six

Perpetual-flowering Carnations

The perpetual-flowering carnation is undoubtedly a greenhouse plant in this country. It is quite true that they will survive remarkably low temperatures, for I have had plants which, planted in the open, survived winter frost of $-13.5°$ C. ($7°$ F.), but no one could have said they were much good afterwards. Plants put outdoors, even in the summer, are nothing like so satisfactory as those kept under glass.

The habit of perpetual-flowering carnations varies quite considerably, some tending to have a shorter and stockier growth than others. There is no reason why one type should be better than the other, but varieties derived from William Sim are tall and are probably the most free-flowering at present.

The majority of amateurs grow perpetual-flowering carnations in pots in a heated greenhouse, and aim to produce blooms throughout the year. A smaller number grow in pots in a cold greenhouse, and aim for bloom in the warmer months only. Professional cut-flower growers, and some amateurs, grow in beds in a heated greenhouse.

The chief advantage of growing in beds is that more blooms are produced per square foot of space, and tying up the plants is far easier. The great disadvantage of beds is the ease with which soil-borne diseases spread. The roots of the plants are not confined as in a pot, and can spread several feet, so if there is any soil-borne disease it is almost impossible to confine it. It is very difficult to make sure that there is no such disease, for these diseases are somewhat peculiar in that they often do not show obvious effects for two years or more, but are passed on during that time in cuttings from the affected plant.

Those who grow in beds must, therefore, be extremely particular as to their stock, and should not take cuttings from plants grown in beds. This means either that special plants must be grown in pots for cuttings, or, as is more usual nowadays, all the plants

83

for putting in the beds are purchased afresh for each planting as rooted cuttings. There are many expert nurserymen who supply such plants, which are grown from specially selected stock, and are tested for disease by laboratory methods. When plants are bought by the thousand, this works out cheaper than doing one's own propagating, but buying fresh stock every year is more expensive on the amateur's scale.

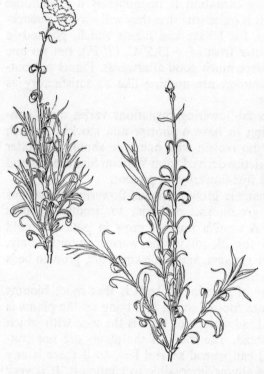

Perpetual-flowering carnations—habit of growth

Left: Short-growing variety. *Right:* Tall growing variety

The amateur should not be deterred by what has been said. If he buys good stock from a reputable source, and grows in pots, he will be able to propagate most of his varieties safely for a considerable time, and if he wishes he can grow some of his plants in beds. The rule is never to propagate from any plant that is unhealthy or has deteriorated in any way, and it is wise never to propagate from plants grown in beds. It is probable that some of his varieties will deteriorate, but they should not be many, and they can be replaced either with the same or a different variety. In practice, most amateurs like to try one or two new varieties each year in any case.

POT CULTIVATION IN A HEATED GREENHOUSE
Cultivation is continuous throughout the year, and a convenient point to begin its description is when most people should begin to grow. The greenhouse and its design and features have already been described in Chapter 3.

The best-sized plant for the beginner is that from a 3- to 3½-inch pot, delivered in April or May. The plant will be what is known as 'stopped and broken', that is the main stem will have been 'stopped', or broken out, at about the seventh joint from the bottom, and five to seven side shoots or 'breaks' will be growing from its joints.

Potting. Some people pot the plants into 6-inch pots as soon as received, but it is really better to pot first into a 4-inch pot, and pot on again into the 6-inch pot when the roots have got well through to the side of the 4-inch pot. The traditional compost described in Chapter 3 should be used, or John Innes No. 2 potting compost. The newly potted plants should be kept in the shade for a couple of days, and lightly syringed over, if the weather is dry, so as to prevent them drying out. After that, they should be watered and stood in full light. When the plants go into the 6-inch pot, a 5-foot cane should be put in to support the plant later on. If the plants are to be flowered for three years, an 8-inch pot should be used.

Throughout the growth of the plant, except for the day or two immediately after potting, enough ventilation should be given to keep the air gently moving about the plants. The air should feel 'buoyant', as gardeners describe it, which is the opposite of close or muggy. Less ventilation is needed at night, but it is a mistake to close down the house early in the afternoon in a misguided attempt to conserve sun heat.

A useful indication is that if condensation of moisture is seen at any time on the inside of the glass, the ventilation has been insufficient.

On most nights in April and May the temperature is not likely to fall below 7° C. (45° F.) inside the greenhouse, but if there is a cold spell it is wise to use a little heat to maintain this minimum temperature.

Stopping. Growth is fairly rapid, and before long some of the side shoots will require stopping; this is known as the second stopping. The correct time to do this is when they are about 7 inches long. Choose the joint nearest the top which shows a clear area of stem between it and the next joint above, and hold

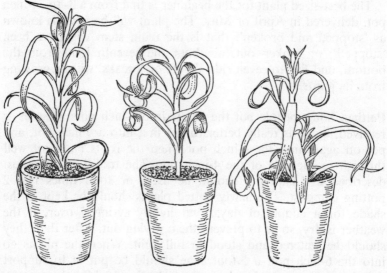

STOPPING A PERPETUAL-FLOWERING CARNATION

Left: Plant ready for stopping. *Centre:* Stopped. *Right:* Previously stopped and breaking at every joint.

it between the thumb and finger of the left hand. Take the top of the shoot in the right hand, and bend it sharply left and right and it should snap off. Stems snap most easily in the early morning after watering the previous day. If the stem does not snap at the joint, do not tug the top out but cut cleanly with a sharp knife as close above the joint as possible.

It is most important to make the break below a clear area of stem, for if merely a bunch of leaves is pulled out of the top, the shoot will grow again from the top in a weakened condition.

The object of the second stopping is twofold. One is to get the plant well furnished with stems before it flowers, and the other is to time the flowering, and spread it. The stopping on a plant should not all be done at once, and each shoot should be dealt with as it becomes ready.

Side shoots that are not stopped will flower at various times in the summer. Those that are stopped will in turn produce side shoots which flower according to the time of stopping. Stopping up to the middle of June produces autumn flowers, and stopping from then to the middle of July produces winter flowers. Stopping in August produces early spring flowers. The normal procedure is to cease stopping at the middle of July. Professionals, who are inclined to use more heat, often stop up to the end of July for winter blooms.

No further stopping is done after the second stopping, but the same effect is produced by cutting the flowers. By the time the flowers are cut the side shoots at the bottom of the stem are clearly seen. Those which are in the right condition to take as cuttings when cuttings are wanted are removed for this purpose, and the rest left to flower in their turn.

Watering and humidity. Watering plants in pots has been dealt with in Chapter 3, but to summarise, it should be said that plenty of water should be given when the plants need it, and no more till the soil is beginning to get dry. If in doubt as to whether water is needed, the best rule is to give it in hot weather, but withhold it in cold weather. This is one of the most difficult points to explain, but it is very soon learned by experience.

It is fairly obvious that if watering the pots is to be restricted, and plenty of ventilation given, the air may become exceedingly dry in hot weather, which may not only wilt the plants, but may also encourage red spider mite (see the chapter on pests and diseases, page 106). We have already noted that perpetual-flowering carnations do not really like being sprayed over at any time, though they tolerate it in summer provided all the moisture has evaporated by the evening. Moreover, water spoils the blooms, so the usual way of keeping the air moist in a greenhouse has great disadvantages for carnations.

This may surprise the older school of growers, who used to spray regularly with salted water. However, this was really to check red spider, and since red spider can now be controlled by chemical means, growers find that keeping the foliage dry is better.

The best method is to stand the pots on a bed of shingle about 2 inches thick. This can be well watered in dry, hot weather, and the floor can be watered as well. In heatwaves this 'damping down', as it is called, may have to be done more than once a day.

Although the bed of shingle may be put on the floor of the greenhouse, a better circulation of air is obtained if it is on a solid staging raised above the floor, even if only a few inches from the ground.

In greenhouses where the ventilation is not quite as good as it should be, some people get the best results by standing the pots on a slatted staging and putting shingle, ashes or old sacks below it, directing the water below the staging.

The pots should not touch each other, for this checks the free flow of air. Moreover, if they did touch each other, there would not be room for the foliage when the plants are fully grown.

Staking. As the plants grow, they should be supported. There is a proprietary support which consists of a wire ring which clips onto the stake and forms a ring of wire round the plant. They are in various sizes to suit the age of the plant, and may be up to 12 inches in diameter, which is about as large as will be required.

Disbudding. Disbudding perpetual-flowering carnations is simple, for all the buds and their stems, except the top or crown bud, are removed. (Recently there has been introduced what is known as the spray carnation, in which the crown bud is removed when it shows colour and the side buds are allowed to develop, producing a spray of small blooms rather like the blooms of annual carnations, though perhaps smaller.) Disbudding is done when the buds and their stems can be easily removed without damage to the flower stem and the crown bud. There is no point in rushing at it too early.

Flowering. Flowers will be produced from the autumn onwards, the exact timing depending on how far growth is advanced and when the second stopping was done. From the time the buds show colour it is important not to get water on them, and if the blooms develop at a time when there is hot sunshine, some shading is needed, as indeed it is during the summer if the heat should be intense. The best form of shading is undoubtedly a greenhouse blind outside the house, because it can be rolled up if the weather becomes dull. However, many people get good results by spraying proprietary shading on the outside of the house.

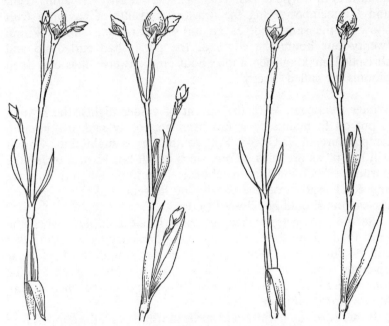

DISBUDDING A PERPETUAL-FLOWERING CARNATION

Left: Two shoots ready for disbudding. *Right:* The same two shoots disbudded.

Home-made shading of whitening or even mud and water is apt to wash off easily, but this can be an advantage if there is a pro-longed spell of dull, rainy weather. The shading should be applied very lightly, using only enough to scatter the sunlight slightly.

It is possible to have a greenhouse blind outside the glass which is rolled up and down by an electric motor controlled by a thermo-stat inside the greenhouse, and no doubt this is a great convenience, but it is not necessary if ordinary care is taken.

Blooms should be cut in the early morning; the next best time is the evening. Their lasting qualities are greatly improved if they stand up to their necks in water for twelve hours or so in a cool place before arranging. Better water uptake is secured if the bottom of the stem is cut on the slant. Carnation flowers should never be sprayed over with water, for water marks them.

Carnation blooms are very susceptible to damage by minute quantities of ethylene gas. This gas is given off by ripening fruit, and I remember seeing the disastrous results of having a fruit show in the same hall as an autumn carnation show. Within twenty-four hours the edges of the petals had curled up and shrivelled, making them look about ten or twelve days old. Such blooms are called 'sleepy'.

Winter treatment. With the advent of colder nights, the heating is put on to maintain, as has been previously said, a minimum temperature of 7° C. (45° F.). Ventilation is maintained, but it will not be as much as before, since it will not be needed for the purpose of cooling the greenhouse. It is important not to have any condensation on the developing flowers, and the shingle on the staging should be allowed to dry.

As the light gets weaker, growth will slow up, and when the buds take a long time to develop, any tendency to split the calyx will be intensified. Wire calyx rings put round the buds near opening time will help to prevent this, though it should be remembered that calyx rings must always be removed when staging blooms for exhibition.

If there are any unduly cold spells in winter, and the temperature falls much below 7° C. (45° F.), growth will be checked, but the plants will make up for it later with a big flush of bloom.

When the days lengthen, growth speeds up and should be vigorous by early spring. From spring onwards, plants which are out of bloom should be examined, and if the roots have formed a mat round the outside of the soil, the plant should be repotted into a larger pot, from a 6-inch pot to an 8-inch pot, or from an 8-inch pot to a 10-inch pot, though the latter is unlikely after the first flowering. If John Innes composts are used, No. 3 is best.

Plants which have not been repotted benefit from weak liquid manure (see Chapter 3, page 50) at fortnightly intervals in summer and monthly intervals in winter.

PROPAGATION BY CUTTINGS

Perpetual-flowering carnations are almost invariably propagated by cuttings. The only exception is when a variety has begun to deteriorate. Some years ago the commercial variety Laddie began to lose vigour, and there was no other suitable variety to take its place. A few enterprising growers propagated it by layers, and were able to go on growing it profitably for a few more years.

Professional growers usually begin to propagate about Christmas time, and continue into January and February. It is sometimes recommended that amateurs should begin in October, but this means that the plant has shortening days ahead of it just when it should be growing most vigorously, and generally it is better to follow the professional example. If, however, there is doubt whether the heating will be enough, there is a lot to be said for early propagation.

Taking cuttings. The cuttings are taken from the lower part of the flowering stem, and there is agreement that young plants produce far better cuttings than old ones. Cuttings should be taken from plants that have been recently watered. Not all the side shoots on the flowering stems make good cuttings. If too small they are dormant, and if they have begun to lengthen for bloom it is too late. Those in between are the correct cuttings. On some varieties they do not reach the right stage until after the bloom has been cut.

It is best not to pull the side shoot off the stem, for this can damage the stem. It is best to cut it off, leaving the bottom, bearing one or two pairs of leaves, on the flowering stem.

The preparation of the cutting, its insertion into the rooting medium, and the hygienic precautions to be taken, are almost the same as has been already described for pink cuttings. The chief difference is that the prepared cutting should have rather more pairs of fully developed leaves, about four to five on the average. Perpetual-flowering carnations are more prone to disease than pinks, so it is even more important to select the parent plant carefully. For example, a plant which persistently bears blooms with split calyxes may be in an early stage of virus infection, and should be rejected for propagation.

Rooting medium. It is necessary to be more particular about the rooting medium than it is with pinks. Sharp sand is the most

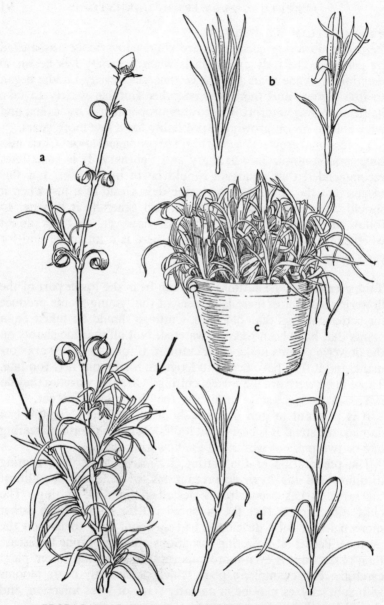

PROPAGATING PERPETUAL-FLOWERING CARNATIONS

(*a*) Flowering stem bearing side shoots. Correct shoots for cuttings indicated by arrows. (*b*) Correct cuttings made from side shoots. (*c*) Pan of newly inserted cuttings. (*d*) Weak shoots unsuitable for cuttings.

favoured, but it must be clean, and if stirring it in water makes the water cloudy, washing is needed. The sand specially sold for propagating is correct as it is, and even if it makes water cloudy, it is all right.

Some people like pure vermiculite, which must be of a horticultural grade, or perlite, but others find it inclined to get too sodden, and difficulty is experienced in getting the cuttings to stand upright. One advantage of vermiculite and perlite is that it is easy to lift the rooted cuttings from them without breaking the roots. Any pot or pan about 3 inches deep will do, and large quantities may be rooted in seed boxes. The cuttings should be inserted 1½ inches apart.

Propagating case. The pots, pans or boxes of cuttings are put into a propagating case, that is to say, a miniature frame inside the greenhouse. Good results can be obtained in a wooden box with a sheet of glass laid on the top. The case should have an inch or so of damp sand in the bottom to help keep a humid atmosphere.

Cuttings root best with a little bottom heat, and the ideal temperatures are 13° C. to 15.5° C. (55° F. to 60° F.) at the bottom and 7° C. to 10° C. (45° F. to 50° F.) at the top. This can be obtained by standing the case above the pipes, or with soil-warming wires if electricity is used. However, cuttings will root well without bottom heat, though they will take longer, and more care must be taken to see that they do not get over-wet.

The propagating case should be kept out of the sun's rays, if any, and the glass kept closed for about two weeks, after which a chink of air should be admitted. Rooting may begin in eighteen days with the quickest rooters, and as soon as the tops begin to grow more air is given, until after four weeks or so the glass is removed altogether. Do not remove the glass until there are definite signs of growth. After the glass is off, the pans are put in the shade on the staging, and after a further ten days or so they are ready for their first potting. They should be lifted very carefully with a small piece of wood or the handle of a kitchen fork, so as not to break the roots.

Potting rooted cuttings. The first potting is into 2½-inch pots, and if the John Innes composts are used, No. 1 is correct. When the roots are well through to the side of the 2½-inch pot, they are potted on into a 3½-inch pot, using the same compost.

During the first or second potting the plants will be ready for their first stopping. When they have produced about nine fully developed pairs of leaves, the top is broken out as previously described under second stopping, leaving seven or eight pairs of leaves remaining. When the side shoots are growing well, we have reached the stage in the cycle of operations with which this description began.

Mist propagation. Perpetual-flowering carnations root exceedingly well in a mist propagator. In fact, they do so well that some growers have dispensed with the use of knives, pulling out pipings of the same length as a normal cutting. When the knack has been learnt this saves a lot of trouble. The bottom heat for mist propagation should be higher than that in a propagating case, namely about 21° C. (70° F.).

Ball watering. Although it is not recommended to beginners, experts sometimes put the rooted cuttings direct into 6-inch pots or beds, and water each plant with small amounts of water on the ball of roots only until it is well established, afterwards watering in the usual way.

Many people do the first potting into pots composed of materials which ultimately disintegrate after the plants are put out. These pots, of course, allow the plants to root through them into the soil. So far I have found only one make of these wholly satisfactory. The great advantage of this type of pot is that it avoids root disturbance. It is also easy to see when the roots show through the sides of the pot. Moreover, they are light and much cleaning of pots is avoided.

POT CULTIVATION IN A COLD HOUSE

I shall not express any opinion on the interminable argument as to whether, if only a cold house is available, it is better to grow border or perpetual-flowering carnations.

There is no doubt that perpetual-flowering carnations will give more blooms on good stems, but they may be spoilt by an exceptionally severe winter. Border carnations, on the other hand, will survive any winter in this country, and produce exquisite blooms.

The cultivation of perpetual-flowering carnations in a cold house is similar to that in a heated house, except that growth almost stops in the winter, although it does not quite do so. Ventilation is just as important as in a heated house.

Summer treatment. The extreme slowness of growth in the winter requires some modification in treatment. The plants are produced in April or May and potted in the usual way, but the second stopping is done only on growths that are ready for it by early June. The remainder are allowed to run up to flower, which they will mostly do from about July onwards. Those that have had the second stopping should carry on the flowering till about October. In that month it is advisable to cut back stems bearing immature buds, for they will not bloom in winter and will spoil.

Winter treatment. During the winter the pots should stand on slatted staging, as this keeps the air drier. Watering should be done carefully, letting the soil get fairly dry between waterings.

Even in the coldest weather some ventilation should be kept on, and this is especially needed after a sunny day to avoid condensation. If the nights are exceptionally cold, putting newspapers over the plants keeps off a great deal of the frost, but the newspapers should not stay on too long. In long cold spells they can be taken off during the day and replaced at night. If the plants do get frosted, they should be sprayed over with very cold water.

When the spring comes, they should be checked to see if they need re-potting into 8-inch pots. They are then allowed to flower when they like. Undeveloped buds are not removed until it is quite clear that they will not flower by December, which they may do if the weather is mild. In the following spring the plants can be planted in the garden, when quite often they will continue to flower during the summer.

Cuttings. Cuttings will not root in a cold house in the winter, so the main batch is taken in August or September, though any that are ready earlier can be taken as they become available. There is quite a chance that there will be winter losses in these cuttings, so plenty should be taken.

There is no fundamental difficulty in growing in a cold house, and there are many amateurs who achieve excellent results. In fact, a large proportion of growers begin in this way, the main difference being that the times at which the various operations are done varies with the season, particularly with home-propagated stock.

GROWING IN BEDS

As has been said, the object of growing in beds is to get more blooms from a given area of greenhouse. The beds may be placed on the soil on the floor of the house, or they may be raised beds. If they are on the floor, it is best to cover the surface with 3-inch draining blocks, and place the growing compost on them.

Raised beds, as their name implies, have a solid bottom above the ground. Both types of bed should have sides tall enough to take 7 inches of the growing compost.

The most permanent material for making the sides, and the base of raised beds, is concrete, and this has the advantage that it is easily cleaned and sterilised between crops. Any other material which is strong enough to hold the weight of the soil will, however, do. Some people use asbestos supported on iron brackets, others use wooden planks, or bricks. Whatever sort of material is used, gaps should be left to ensure free drainage. Very often a gap is left down the middle of a solid base, or the middle can be raised a couple of inches to provide a slight slope down to the sides, which can either have plentiful drainage holes, or be only loosely fitted to the base. It is worth mentioning that wood should never be treated with creosote. A good wood preservative is a proprietary green preservative consisting of copper naphthanate in kerosene, which should be used according to the maker's instructions.

The only limit on the width of the bed is that it must be possible to reach each plant in it easily, and it is not wise to have the paths too narrow—2 feet is about the minimum. Most beds are about 3½ feet wide, and 4½ feet should be regarded as a maximum.

The soil for the beds is the same as for potting. If the John Innes compost is used, the amount of fertiliser should be adjusted so that it is halfway between No. 1 and No. 2, usually called

No. 1½ by professional growers. This is not generally sold ready made up, but, of course, can be prepared by mixing together equal parts of No. 1 and No. 2.

Planting. Amateurs usually plant out in beds in March to May, using stopped and broken plants from 3½-inch pots; in fact, at the same stage as they would normally go into 4- or 6-inch pots for pot culture. Some professional growers, however, save a vast amount of labour by planting rooted cuttings direct into the beds, using ball watering until the plants are big enough for the whole bed to be watered. These growers often do not propagate their own stock, but buy plants by the thousand from specialist firms, who, if notified in advance, can deliver to the day required. In fact, plants of any size can be planted out from February to May, provided care is taken to water only the balls of roots until the roots have spread right through the beds.

The usual planting distance is 8 inches apart, both between plants and rows, but the plants are never staggered as this interferes with supporting them. Another way is to plant in double rows, 7 inches between the plants and 4 inches between the rows, and then a space of 10 inches before the next double row. Each plant is supported by an 8- to 9-inch stick and a ring tie.

Supports. The plants are later on supported by stretching wires lengthwise along the bed, and tying string to the wires across the beds, so as to form squares of wire and string in which the plants grow. The supports for the wires must be substantial, and may consist of stout upright iron stakes driven into the ground or embedded in concrete at each end of the bed. To these uprights cross bars are fixed at 6-inch intervals, so that rows of wires can be stretched at intervals of 6 inches in height along the beds. If the bed is a long one, supports (which need not be heavy) are fixed across the bed at 10- to 12-foot intervals to prevent the wires sagging. The distance between the wires averages 8 inches, but if the double row method of planting is used the wires run between the rows. The cross strings, which are tied to the outside wires and looped over the wires between, should enclose each plant at a distance of 4 to 5 inches on the lower wires, increasing to the full planting distance on the top wires, which should be about 6 feet above the surface of the bed.

C.A.P.—4

General care. Watering is required less frequently in beds than in pots, and is usually done with a hose without a nozzle, directing the water close to the soil, so as not to wet the foliage unduly. Feeding is not usually done until after the first crop of blooms has been gathered, that is to say, about six to nine months after planting.

Apart from what has been said in the foregoing, cultivation does not differ from that in pots.

Bed cultivation is usually based on growing the plants for two years, but with feeding they will go on for three years, though two years is recommended.

When the beds are cleared, they should be washed and sterilised. With beds built upon the ground, the soil under the drainage blocks should also be sterilised. Steam sterilisation is rarely used by amateurs, but there are proprietary sterilising solutions based on cresylic acid, which are effective and safe, if the makers' directions are strictly followed. Sterilising the compost in the beds and using it again is not recommended for carnations.

SAND CULTURE

Sand (including gravel) culture consists of growing plants in clean sand or gravel and supplying nutrient solutions during growth. It has the advantage that no soil pests or diseases are introduced into the greenhouse, but it cannot, of course, check the spread of disease from one plant to another. Some very good results have been obtained by growing perpetual-flowering carnations in sand. The methods are described in books on soilless culture, or in the instructions for the use of proprietary preparations. One very good proprietary preparation is merely sprinkled on the top of the sand at stated intervals and watered in.

RING CULTURE

The great advantage of ring culture is that watering and feeding are so easy that even a beginner can hardly make a mistake. Planting is done into bottomless 5-inch pots standing on a bed or 8-inch pots of ashes, vermiculite or granulated pumice stone. The 5-inch pot is filled with John Innes No. 1 potting compost, leaving about $\frac{1}{2}$ inch for watering. The lower pot or bed is kept well watered the whole time, so there is no problem of when to water.

At first the plant in the 5-inch pot is watered carefully in the usual way, and before long the roots grow down into the wet medium in the lower pot or bed. They then grow rapidly into the medium, and take their water supply from it. Feeding is carried out by filling the 5-inch pot to the brim with a liquid fertiliser, a high potash one being most suitable. This is done once a week in summer, but less often in winter, for the soil must not be continuously wet in the 5-inch pot. Every three weeks to a month would be about right.

The only disadvantage is that if 8-inch pots are used, they take up a fair amount of room and are difficult to move about. If beds are used, pests or diseases will not, of course, be brought in with the medium, but soil- or root-borne disease can spread from plant to plant just as it does in a normal bed.

Ring culture is not, in fact, used very much by growers, but its advantages should not be overlooked, and to my mind more people should try it.

Chapter Seven

Growing from Seed

When we say that a plant does or does not come true from seed, we are always using the phrases in a relative sense. Annual carnations, such as the Chabaud and Charm types, come very true to habit, form, and shape of flower, and some strains to colour, so we can rely on them to produce a batch of plants sufficiently uniform for bedding out, but, in fact, they do vary somewhat from each other. Border and perpetual-flowering carnations and pinks, on the other hand, produce an extremely variable batch of seedlings. Even good seed from a reputable nurseryman, which is the only kind worth growing, produces many inferior plants, but there is always the chance of a really good one, which is what makes it so fascinating. Moreover, seedlings are often extremely vigorous and healthy, and some people may prefer some of the unconventional flowers that appear.

The method of sowing and pricking out is the same for all, the only difference being in the time at which it is done, and, of course, the subsequent treatment.

Sowing. The John Innes seed compost is ideal, but a mixture of 2 parts loam and 1 part sharp sand is quite satisfactory. In fact, any compost suitable for the seeds of the majority of plants will do. Pots, pans or seed boxes, according to the number of seeds in the batch, are all quite suitable, and a single crock over the drainage hole of a pot or pan is enough. Fine soil will be needed for covering the seeds, and it is a good idea to sift some and put it aside while filling the containers, putting the coarse soil left in the sieve in the bottom of the containers. A small box with the bottom removed, and a piece of ordinary perforated zinc tacked in its place, makes an excellent sieve.

The container should be filled to within $\frac{1}{2}$ inch of the top with soil, which is levelled off and gently pressed down. It should be

well watered and the seeds can be sown at once. Even with sterilised soil, damping-off disease may attack. This is a fungus which
creeps along the surface of the soil and kills the main stem of the
seedling, causing it to fall over and die. There is no cure for an
affected seedling, but the disease is easily prevented by using
Cheshunt compound for watering the containers. This is so cheap
that it is not worth compounding at home, and various proprietary
brands give full directions for use.

The seeds are best spaced out about $\frac{1}{4}$ inch apart, and should
be covered with about $\frac{1}{16}$ to $\frac{1}{8}$ inch of fine soil, not more. A sheet
of glass is laid across the top of the container, and the container
is placed in a temperature of about 16° C. (60° F.). Germination
takes about seven to ten days, after which the sheet of glass is
removed.

If the temperature is controlled, pricking out into John Innes
No. 1 potting compost is done as soon as all the seedlings have
fully developed their cotyledons or seed leaves, but in a cold house
or frame it is safer to wait until the first pair of true leaves are
about $\frac{1}{2}$ inch long. The pricking out distance is $1\frac{1}{2}$ inches apart.

A word of warning. Seeds of dianthus are much more brittle
than nearly all other seeds, and care should be taken not to crack
them in handling. On no account must seedlings, or seeds that
have begun to germinate, be allowed to dry out.

At some stage the seedlings must be hardened off, that is to
say, gradually accustomed to the conditions in which they are to
grow and flower, which is usually cooler and drier than the place
where they germinated and were pricked out. This is dealt with
separately below.

Annual carnations. Although it is possible to sow annual carnations
in April in a cold house, they will be very late in flowering, so the
usual practice is to sow in a heated greenhouse in February. After
pricking out, the plants must be watched to see that they do not
grow leggy, which indicates that the heat is too great in relation
to light. About the middle of April the plants are removed to a
cold frame, which is kept close for a day or two. The light is
then gradually opened to admit more air, and after ten days or
so is removed, being replaced only if frost threatens.

They are planted out 9 to 12 inches apart at the end of April
or the beginning of May in the South, and up to about a fortnight

later in the North. If well hardened off, a touch of ground frost will not harm them.

Perpetual-flowering carnations. The important point with perpetual-flowering carnation seedlings is to get them to bloom in the late summer and autumn, so that the undesirables can be weeded out before they occupy valuable greenhouse space in the winter. Sowing is, therefore, begun as early in the New Year as possible, and not later than February.

Since the winter temperature in the greenhouse will be too low, a specially heated propagating case is needed, in which a temperature of 16° C. (60° F.) can be maintained. If the house has hot-water pipes, the case can be placed over a hot pipe, and if electric heating is used, the case can be heated with soil-warming wires.

Hardening off consists of accustoming the seedlings to the normal temperature of the greenhouse, and is accomplished by reducing the temperature of the propagating case, and admitting more air over the course of a fortnight or so. A point not to be overlooked is that the propagating case may not hold all the plants after pricking out, so it may be necessary to harden off before pricking out. In that case it is best to let the plants get a bit larger than usual before pricking out. Many growers prefer to prick out into 2-inch pots rather than boxes.

After the seedlings are potted up, their culture is the same as a plant from a cutting, except that they are not stopped, and the central stem is allowed to run up to bloom. Any that have not done so by October are probably too slow growing to be any use, and can be discarded with the other poor plants.

It is important to give all the seedlings the best possible treatment, because if the good ones are neglected in any way the effects will probably persist throughout the life of the variety.

Border carnations and pinks. Although a minimum temperature of 16° C. (60° F.) cannot be maintained in a cold house or frame, conditions there become suitable for sowing border carnations and pinks about the end of the first week in April in the South, and two to three weeks later as we go further north. There seems to be an upper, as well as a lower, limit of temperature for good germination, and if the temperature in the greenhouse is likely to run up to 27° C. (80° F.), or over, as it may do later in the season, it is better to place the containers in the shade of a north wall outdoors (with the sheet of glass over them, of course).

Seed can be sown in a bed outdoors, but in this case losses from various causes are inclined to be high.

Pricking out is as usual. If the seedlings are in a cold house, they are best hardened off by placing in a cold frame and increasing the air over a period of a week or so till the light is taken off permanently. If there is no cold frame available, they should be watered and stood outdoors in the shade for an hour or two one day, the whole day the next day, and the third day left out permanently. If the weather is dull and damp, the containers can merely be put outdoors and left there without further trouble.

A week or so later the containers are placed in a sunny place, and planting out can begin after a few days.

Normally the plants are left to flower only for the following season, when the good ones are propagated and the rest thrown away. Since the plants are to remain only one year, planting distances can be as little as 9 inches apart for border carnations and 6 to 7 inches for pinks.

A method of getting large quantities of bloom for cut flowers is to plant border carnation seedlings about 15 inches apart in a reserve bed. The plants are allowed to bloom for two years, and after the second blooming the side shoots are layered into the ground and left without severing them from the parent plant. Great quantities of bloom are obtained in the third year.

The old type of pink can be grown in just the same way as a border carnation, but the modern type often sends up a flower stem in the autumn of the year the seedlings are planted, or very early in the following spring. Some growers say you should not stop seedlings, so as to judge them at the first opportunity. I am sure this is wrong for two reasons, namely that the first blooms of modern pinks are not typical of the usual blooms, and it is just as important to judge the habit of a pink as its bloom. The habit of a pink which would normally be stopped cannot be properly judged on an unstopped plant.

Selecting the seedlings. Although it is possible to eliminate worthless plants on their first blooming, it does not follow that those with good blooms are good plants, and this applies to border and perpetual-flowering carnations and pinks. The border carnations should be layered, and the other two propagated by cuttings, at least twice before a sound judgment can be given.

Beginners should remember that their best seedling may not be really good compared to existing varieties, nor should they be surprised if nurserymen are reluctant to give their seedlings a free trial. The nurseryman has seedlings of his own, and it costs quite a lot in labour, materials and so on to test them. I remember going with the late Montagu Allwood through a field of his seedling pinks, putting sticks to mark those worthy of propagation. He said: 'Don't forget, every stick that goes in will cost me £10,' and that was several years ago.

The best thing to do is to put any seedling in which one has confidence before the appropriate committee of the Royal Horticultural Society. Those that receive awards will probably be tested by a nurseryman if he is asked to do so.

Chapter Eight

Pests and Diseases

If a complete list of pests and diseases which could attack carnations and pinks were made, it would be alarming, but the alarm would not be justified, because with ordinary common sense and good cultivation very few of the many pests and diseases actually do attack.

If an attack occurs, it usually means that some kind of chemical will have to be used. It must always be remembered that when dealing with horticultural chemicals the words 'poisonous' and 'non-poisonous' are relative terms, and all of them should be treated with care. There is a government scheme which gives approval to certain chemical preparations, but it is a voluntary scheme and there is nothing to prevent the selling of unapproved products. Approved products bear on the label a special mark, consisting of a capital A with a crown above it, and below it the words 'Agricultural Chemicals Approval Scheme'. This does not mean that all such chemicals are safe for the amateur, but it does mean that, among other things, the label states clearly any special precautions needed.

A list of approved products can be obtained free from the Ministry of Agriculture, Fisheries and Food (Publications), Tolcarne Drive, Pinner, Middlesex.

Always read the label carefully, and carry out the directions exactly. Do not use household spoons or similar containers for measuring—measures are cheap enough at any chemist's shop. Never 'add a bit more for luck'. Do not inhale or swallow dusts, sprays or smokes. Wash your hands thoroughly after handling chemicals. Keep chemicals (and even the empty containers) away from children and pets, preferably in a locked cupboard. Be careful to keep them away from bees, fish, and wild birds. Do not relax precautions even if the label bears such words as 'safe', 'harmless' or 'non-poisonous'.

There is a special point about sprays used on carnations. Carnations and pinks are in general very resistant to damage by the actual active chemicals in the sprays, but all liquid sprays contain spreaders, and sometimes emulsifiers to keep the active chemical in solution. These sometimes dissolve or remove the natural waxy coating of the leaves, and cause harm. Thus, wherever possible, the chemicals should be applied as dusts, smokes or wettable powders. If a spreader is necessary it should not be soap. Most proprietary sprays contain their own spreader, so there is no choice, but if anyone makes his own spray, the safest spreader is saponin, a natural alkaloid, used at the rate of 1 ounce to 50 gallons of the solution.

PESTS

Returning to the pests, they may be classified as leaf suckers, leaf eaters, and root pests.

Aphis. The most dangerous pest is aphis, or greenfly, not because of the actual damage it causes by sucking the sap, though this can be severe if unchecked, but because it spreads virus diseases, for which, generally speaking, the amateur has no cure. Viruses are much more plentiful and dangerous in the case of perpetual-flowering carnations, and since these are grown in greenhouses which can be closed up, BHC smokes are the most effective means of controlling greenfly. Used every fourteen days, they should keep the house clear.

Outdoor plants are often not attacked at all, and if they are a BHC or lindane spray should soon clear them. Using a liquid spray once in a while should not damage the waxy covering of the leaves unduly. This can also be used on border carnations grown in a house that cannot be closed down. Systemic insecticides give protection for a number of days, and of these, sprays containing menazon are effective and safe for the plants but menazon should not be used on plants intended for producing pollen or seed.

Red spider. The pest known as red spider is neither red nor a spider, being a very small brown mite—in America it is called the two-spot-mite. Although a serious pest of fruit trees and other outdoor plants, it hardly ever attacks carnations and pinks in the open. The old remedy was to spray with lime sulphur, and this can still be used in a house that cannot be closed down. In a house that can be closed down azobenzene smokes are effective, and two treatments with a five-day interval are advised.

Hot, dry conditions favour this pest, and well-ventilated houses with sufficient damping down check it considerably. It spreads very slowly from plant to plant, so all the plants should be watched, since a severe attack on one or two plants might be missed. When numerous, it spins fine webs under the leaves.

Frog hopper. The larva of the frog hopper sucks the stem and covers itself with a mass of froth, whence it is called soapy-blight, cuckoo-spit, or in America, spittle-bug. It is a common pest on many garden plants. It causes considerable damage to carnations and pinks, distorting the flower stems, but is soon settled by a BHC spray applied so as to wash off the froth. It is rare under glass.

Thrips. This is a minute black sucking insect that does much damage to many plants. It damages carnation and pink blooms by sucking the miniature petals, coloured varieties showing a white spot on the petals when they expand. DDT used as a dust or spray made from wettable powder is effective outdoors, and in a closed house DDT or BHC smokes are effective. In bad years treatment may have to be as often as once a week.

Caterpillars. The chief leaf-eaters are caterpillars of the tortrix moth or the tomato moth, though the dot moth may sometimes attack. Leaves of cuttings and seedlings are sometimes eaten by woodlice (called sow bugs in America). The remedy for all of them is DDT, as a smoke in a closed house, or outdoors as a spray made from wettable powder or as a dust.

General precautions. From the remedies described above, it will be seen that few chemicals are needed to control all pests of the stems and leaves. For perpetual-flowering carnations grown in a house that can be closed, it is best to prevent pests by fumigating every fourteen days with a combined DDT and BHC smoke, since this cannot damage the foliage, using azobenzene smoke as well if red spider appears.

Outdoors, or in a house that cannot be closed, it is best to watch carefully for an attack, and then apply the appropriate remedy as a spray or dust.

Carnation flies. Carnation flies, of which there are more than one species, can operate at almost any time of the year and are extremely difficult to control, but they never seem to attack plants under glass. Outdoors, the maggots burrow inside the leaves and often pass from the leaves into the stem. They mainly attack seedlings just after they have been hardened off, and layers of border carnations in the open. If the maggot gets into the stem of a border carnation or an old-type pink, the next year's flowering will be prevented, but a modern-type pink will flower as if it had been stopped.

If carnation flies are about, a method of prevention is to lift plants intended for layering and plant in pots, doing the layering under glass.

To prevent attack on seedlings, dusting, for the first four weeks after they are put outdoors, every week with BHC powder, seems effective. After plants are attacked, one method is to pinch off all leaves which show the white tracks of the maggot, and if the stem is attacked, to stab down with a needle to kill the grub. Those used to handling poisonous sprays often have good results with nicotine, but, naturally, it requires careful use.

Soil pests. As has been mentioned, the most effective insecticide for killing biting and sucking insects in the soil is no longer available, but DDT and BHC may provide good substitutes. Composts which are sterilised, such as the John Innes mixtures, should not contain any pests.

DISEASES

It is easy to become over-anxious about diseases, but going to the other extreme, and leaving diseases until they affect the entire collection, is even worse. The sensible thing to do is to watch carefully any plant that seems to be growing badly, and if it shows definite signs of disease, to deal with it at once. If it goes on growing badly without showing definite signs of disease, it is not worth keeping and might just as well be thrown out.

In fact, the chief sufferers from diseases are the growers of commercial cut flowers. The reason is that they grow vast numbers of plants of only a few varieties. Different varieties vary considerably in their resistance to various diseases, and the diseases themselves have different strains which vary in their ability to attack different varieties. Also, it seems that the diseases are capable of producing variants which will attack a variety hitherto resistant. Thus if a disease strain or variant establishes on one plant of a carnation variety, it has a free run on all other plants of the same variety, and can spread like wildfire.

The amateur, on the other hand, usually has a very mixed collection of varieties, and most of his plants are likely to show resistance to some extent to the particular disease if it occurs.

In my view it does not do the amateur much good to spend time diagnosing the exact disease, for example the difference between *Fusarium* and *Verticillium* (*Phialophora*) wilt, if all he can do in either case is to burn the plant and any cuttings taken from it. It is better to divide the diseases between curable and incurable ailments, and try to prevent them all and cure the curable ones.

It is fairly obvious that any plant material affected by disease should be kept away from healthy plants, but it should also be remembered that damaged tissue of *any* plant tends to give off ethylene gas, which, as we have noticed, prematurely ages carnation blooms and causes them to go 'sleepy'. Therefore, a diseased plant of any kind, pulled up weeds, or cut foliage, and so on, must never be allowed to remain in a greenhouse.

Soil which has been used for growing carnations in the greenhouse should not be put in places from which soil may be taken for further use, at any rate until four or five years have elapsed.

General cleanliness in respect of tools, greenhouses and the like is of great importance and pots should be thoroughly scrubbed before re-use. A soil steriliser based on cresylic acid is a good disinfectant for general use, though it must be kept away from growing crops.

Incurable diseases. The wilts and rots which may attack carnations are serious and highly infectious. They are caused by fungi or bacteria which, unfortunately, may remain for two years or more in the plant without showing any signs, so that it is possible to carry them over on apparently healthy cuttings or layers. They mostly attack perpetual-flowering carnations, but sometimes attack border carnations and less often pinks. The usual sign is a sudden wilting of the whole or part of the plant. Many of them can affect the soil or be passed on by contact with the roots. Affected plants should be removed and burnt, and a sharp watch kept on other plants in the border or greenhouse.

Plants grown outdoors may infect the bed in which the plants are growing, so changing the site frequently is a wise precaution. To decide whether it is necessary to change the site, it is important to distinguish the specific carnation rots and wilts from the ordinary stem rot, which is caused by common organisms in the soil. These may attack any carnation or pink that has been planted too deeply or is growing in badly drained soil, and a properly planted carnation subsequently put in the same soil and properly drained will not be affected. Ordinary stem rot is usually noticed in winter and spring, and the whole plant dies without any change of colour. The specific rots, however, usually attack in warm weather, and cause the foliage to change to yellow or straw colour, or sometimes affect only part of the plant, and if these occur, the site must be changed for the next planting.

The virus diseases are more insidious, and usually cause a slow decline of the plant, perhaps accompanied by spots or streaks on the foliage and poor blooms and split calyces. Some viruses have no effect on the health of some varieties, which then act as carriers which can infect other plants. Viruses are transmitted through cuttings and layers of infected plants, but the chief way in which they spread is by being carried by greenfly, so control of this pest is essential.

Although not practical for the amateur, it is interesting to note that most, if not all, carnation viruses have been eliminated in laboratories by either or both of two methods, namely growing for one or two months at 38° C. (100° F.), and propagating by taking a minute piece of the growing tip ($\frac{1}{2}$ to 1 millimetre long), and culturing it in a special solution.

Curable diseases. The commonest carnation diseases are caused by fungi, and it so happens that the prevention and cure of nearly all of them are the same.

The one which has the most easily recognisable signs is carnation rust. It can attack perpetual-flowering carnations in a greenhouse at any time, but border carnations usually show signs in late autumn or early winter. Pinks are rarely affected. In certain districts, especially near towns where there is sulphur pollution of the air, the disease appears to attack only young stock brought from somewhere else, and the infection does not spread. Nevertheless, precautions should be taken even here if it is seen. If an infected border carnation is obtained in spring, showing no signs of the disease, and it is layered in summer, the layers usually also show the disease in the autumn. The signs are raised chocolate-brown spots, which burst open and release the spores, which look rather like cocoa powder.

There are various moulds and mildews which attack the leaves, often causing spots or purplish markings.

Under glass, attacks of all these fungi are favoured by damp conditions, and the spores are spread by splashing water about. Stagnant moisture on the leaves helps the spores to germinate and penetrate the plant. Preventive measures are, therefore, good cultivation and ample ventilation.

Outdoors, moisture is not under control, and the diseases are liable to be spread by rain and wind, the rain helping the spores to attack. One, *Alternaria dianthi*, can sometimes cause hardly any signs on the plants outdoors, but as soon as cuttings are placed in the moist atmosphere of the propagating frame, they become covered with a grey mould resembling the botrytis mould so deadly to other plants.

The old cure for all these fungi was dusting or spraying with sulphur sprays, but thiram was found to be more effective, and some nurserymen use thiram sprays on all cuttings as a precaution. More recently zineb has been found by some growers to be even more effective than thiram for carnation rust. Captan and dinocap are sometimes effective, and changing fungicides from time to time prevents resistant strains of disease from building up.

PHYSIOLOGICAL DISORDERS

Although persistent calyx splitting may be due to a virus, it can be caused by alterations in temperature, extreme variations in soil moisture, or anything that causes alternation of fast and slow growth. These conditions can also cause the leaves at the tip of the growth to stick together. The remedy is to try to promote even growth.

To sum up, the best way to avoid all diseases is good general cultivation, which includes strict cleanliness and never propagating from any but the best and healthiest plants.

Chapter Nine

Breeding New Varieties

The breeding of new varieties is one of the most fascinating occupations for any gardener. The thrill of waiting to see results is, to my mind, unequalled in gardening pleasures, and even if there are far more disappointments than successes, a real success wipes out all memories of failures.

Strictly speaking, any seedling of a border carnation, perpetual-flowering carnation or pink could be called a new variety, but there is no point in so doing and naming it unless it is an advance on existing varieties. The art and science of breeding is a big subject, and even elementary treatment requires a book to itself. It would not be worth writing such a book on dianthus alone, for much of it would be common to other plants. I have written an elementary book on the art, namely *Plant Breeding for Gardeners* (Collingridge). I propose in this chapter to start the beginner on his way, and if he gets interested, he can follow the matter up in that and other books.

The great thing is to begin, for even a novice can have a startling success, and beat someone who has been at it for years. In this lies much of the fascination.

Crossing. The technique of crossing two varieties together is easy. Shortly after the flower opens the anthers, which are little bags about $\frac{1}{8}$ inch long on the end of stalks called filaments, burst open and discharge the pollen. Later in the life of the flower, usually seven to ten days later, the styles develop and stick up above the petals, curving at the tip. (The flowers in the painting referred to in Chapter 1 had reached this stage.) When ready to receive the pollen, the stigmatic surface, which is on the outside of the curve of the style, shows numerous minute hairs, each with a glistening drop of fluid at the tip (a magnifying glass is needed to see this). Fundamentally, crossing is transferring freshly shed pollen from one variety to the ripe stigma of another variety, allowing the seed

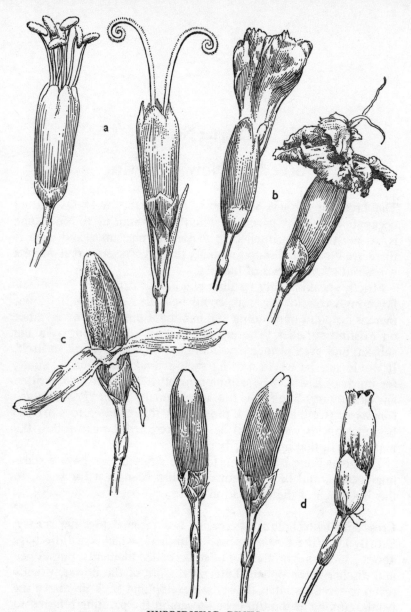

HYBRIDISING PINKS

(*a*) Flowers with petals removed to show parts. *Left:* Anthers ripe on young flower. *Right:* Stigmas ripe on old flower. (*b*) *Left:* Collapse of petals on fertilised flower. *Right:* Bloom withered without fertilisation. (*c*) Swelling seedpod with calyx torn down to avoid water collecting. (*d*) Ripening seedpods. *Left:* Yellowing at tip indicates ripening, can be gathered. *Centre:* Tip of pod just opening. Must be gathered. *Right:* Pod opened. Should have been gathered before and some seeds may have been lost.

to develop, and sowing it. The simplest way to transfer pollen is to pull off a newly burst anther with a pair of tweezers, and wipe it gently upwards along the stigmatic surface.

The stigma should remain dry and protected from moisture for at least six hours. If the pollen has taken, the petals collapse in a typical way twelve to forty-eight hours after pollination. As soon as this happens, the calyx should be torn open on the under side to prevent moisture collecting, which might rot the seed pod. The petals should be pulled out as soon as they have shrivelled enough to pull out easily, and the calyx should be removed entirely.

The pod will soon swell up, and five to six weeks later begins to grow brown at the tip. When the brown extends about a third of the way down the pod, the pod should be gathered, placed in a paper bag and kept for a week or so in a dry place, when it should be gently broken open and the seeds extracted. When quite dry they can be stored in packets in a tin until they are sown as described in Chapter 7. Any outstanding seedling is then propagated by layers or cuttings in the usual way. (The breeding of new strains of annual carnations is rather more complicated, for the strain has to be fixed to breed true, and this is not dealt with here.)

Precautions. There are two more questions to deal with. Must the anthers of the seed-producing flower be removed to make sure it is not fertilised by its own pollen, and must it be protected from bees or other insects? The test is to leave some flowers on the plant without pollination, and see if the petals collapse in the typical way. If they do not, the precautions are not necessary.

If they do, remove the anthers before they burst from some flowers (which is called emasculation), and then wait and see what happens. If these flowers do not collapse, it is fairly certain that the collapse of the other flowers is due to their own pollen, and emasculation is needed. If the flowers which have been emasculated collapse, it is fairly certain that insects are at work, and they must be excluded by placing muslin or nylon bags over the flowers.

It is almost universally agreed that border carnations and pinks very rarely, or never, set seed with their own pollen, and insects pollinate them only in some districts. Most breeders of perpetual-flowering carnations are careful to emasculate their plants, but usually do not protect them from insects, though in some districts they take steps to exclude insects from the greenhouse, either with proprietary repellants or netting over the ventilators. As the anthers of perpetual-flowering carnations are often well down among the petals, removing them involves removing the petals. British breeders normally remove all the petals, but American breeders usually leave the outer petals to act as pollination indicators by collapsing if the pollen takes.

Orthodox scientific breeding is based on crossing two varieties together, and then crossing their offspring among each other, because many characters are hidden in the first generation, appearing only in the second. In America the inheritance of flower colour has been investigated carefully in perpetual-flowering carnations, but it does not follow that *all* varieties will conform to the published results.

A difficulty in using orthodox methods with carnations and pinks is that they are so sensitive to the ill-effects of inbreeding that the second generation plants usually are weakly, and since health and vigour are the most important attributes of the plants they are difficult to judge. However, if one has two different strains weakened by inbreeding, crossing them together restores vigour, so this is a way out.

Nevertheless, the most successful practical breeders use another method. They make a number of crosses, recording them with great care, and after a time get to know the good parents, namely those which are most likely to pass on good attributes to their offspring. They then cross the good parents together, proceeding on their acquired knowledge of what each is likely to pass on to the offspring. If they do not get what they want, they cross a seedling from one pair of good parents with a seedling of another pair of good parents, thus avoiding inbreeding.

Recording results. Keeping records is easy. As each cross is made, it is given a number which is written on a tie-on label attached to the seed-bearing bloom. The number is recorded in a stud book giving full particulars of the cross. It is advisable to make reciprocal crosses in each case, that is to say, using each parent both as a pollen and a seed parent, because often the pollen takes one way better than the other. Contrary to popular belief, and in accordance with scientific theory, the inheritance of characters by the offspring does not appear to be affected by whether a particular plant is the seed or the pollen parent.

Although crossing is mainly done to improve the characteristics of the flowers, it is absolutely vital that the new variety should be healthy, vigorous and easy to cultivate. This is the point on which most beginners err. It is no use having beautiful flowers if the plant is unhealthy or difficult to grow. Using poor-growing or disease-susceptible plants as parents, can show its effect generations later, and may wreck years of careful work.

Luck and skill. Since nobody can be quite sure what will result from a cross which has not been tried before, it is obvious that chance must play a part in getting good results. As has been said, a beginner may have a striking success at a first attempt, but naturally this is rare. More often, success comes only after much methodical and patient effort, though since chance is always present there is no guarantee that the effort will be rewarded. Some people might say that, the greater the skill of the breeder, the less chance enters into it, but I prefer to say that skill consists in getting the odds in your favour.

Selection. Since the mechanical details of crossing plants are simple and easily mastered, it is clear that skill must be acquired in some other direction, and that direction is selection. Selection is applied twice, namely in selecting the right parents, and later on in selecting the seedlings resulting from the cross. As has been mentioned, in course of time a store of information is built up concerning the value of particular plants as parents, but we must make a start somewhere before we can acquire this information, and this is where selection of parents saves much random and wasted effort.

As each cross can result in quite a number of seeds, there may be many seedlings, and it will be necessary to select carefully those which are worth growing on and propagating by cuttings or layers as the case may be. As mentioned in Chapter 7, the selection of perpetual-flowering carnation seedlings should be completed before they take up valuable space in the greenhouse in winter, but border carnations and pinks can be left until the ground is wanted for other purposes, because even the poorer seedlings will still give a good display in the garden.

Observation. The difference between a good plant breeder and a bad one really lies in the extent to which he develops his powers of observation. This does not come all at once, but it is my firm belief that anyone who loves flowers is willing to take a certain amount of trouble, has some common sense, and is willing to train his powers of observation, can be a good plant breeder. Since it is highly unlikely that anyone without these qualities would have read as far as this, it is fairly safe to assume that the reader can be a good plant breeder if he wishes.

Obviously the first thing one looks at is the flower. A valuable way to train oneself to observe flowers is to exhibit at shows in competition with other growers, but naturally nobody expects great success in competitions at first. However, it is consoling to know that much more is usually learned by failure than by success. If one cannot compete, a good deal can be learned by studying other people's exhibits.

Points to consider. Although the flower is what catches the eye, in fact some of the other characteristics of the plant are more important. As has been said, good health and freedom from diseases and pests are of first importance, for without them the other qualities of the plant are of little use. Next I should put good strong growth and freedom of flowering, and after that excellence of flower and scent combined with a good strong stem. Ease of propagating by cuttings or layers probably comes next, and after that a number of minor but still important points. Does the flower last well when cut? Does the calyx tend to split? Does the flower fade in strong light? If a pink, must it be staked? Does the plant produce enough side shoots, or is there a tendency for it to flower itself to death? Do the flowers come all at once, or is there a steady succession? What proportion of the flowers are fully up to standard? If an outdoor plant, does the flower resist rain damage? Is the plant damaged by the usual sprays? Is the seedling better than existing varieties?

It is clear that most of these points can only be observed by careful study of the plant at various stages of its growth, and everyone should make a habit of examining his plants closely at frequent intervals, and comparing one with another. Comparison is probably the best way of developing observation.

Making a start. I again strongly urge that the beginner should not delay his first attempts until he has acquired skill in observation.

He should plunge right into crossing at the earliest opportunity, for not only may he strike lucky at an early attempt, but also comparing seedlings with their parents is probably the best way of acquiring knowledge of breeding.

Though no substitute for practical experience, reading about the principles of genetics and the practice of plant breeding can be a great help as skill increases, particularly in avoiding wasted effort. The only danger in reading too much about genetics is that it makes plant breeding seem more difficult than it really is. Reading about practical breeding is helpful but it should not be confined to carnations and pinks, for often a difficult problem in breeding them can be solved by knowing how a similar problem has been solved in a totally different plant. The most helpful other plants to study are those which, like carnations and pinks, are perennials which have been extensively bred for a long time, and show the bad effects of inbreeding very rapidly. Examples are roses and gladioli.

Further hints. Although, as has been pointed out, it is a principle of genetics that many characteristics disappear in the first generation and reappear in the second, yet, in plants which have been extensively bred, such characteristics do not always completely disappear in the first generation, so that minute examination can sometimes reveal traces of a desired characteristic in a seedling. This seedling can then be crossed with another seedling of different parentage showing the same traces, thus bringing out the desired characteristic without inbreeding.

As time goes on, the selection of parents by their visible characteristics will gradually be supplanted by selecting them by their performance as parents, and from then rapid progress should be made.

Chapter Ten

Some Suggested Varieties

It will be remembered that in Chapter 1 reasons were given why it is better to rely on the advice of a reputable nurseryman rather than on lists of varieties, but a beginner might still be somewhat bewildered by the choice offered. To help him, therefore, I have compiled lists of varieties particularly with the beginner in mind. For example, in the list of perpetual-flowering carnations all but one of the excellent varieties derived from William Sim have been omitted, simply because I think they are rather too tall for a beginner to manage easily.

Although most plants in the lists have been in the catalogues for some time, there is no guarantee that they will continue to be available for long. Any of them could disappear from commerce in a short time, as for example did some excellent scarlet border carnations on the introduction of Fiery Cross. If they do, it is not because they were bad, but because something better has come along.

The lists, of course, reflect my personal preferences, and someone else might compile totally different and equally good lists. I must repeat that it is essential to get good stocks from a reputable nurseryman. Such nurserymen often also offer special collections at an inclusive price, and this is another way for the beginner to choose varieties, for these collections are usually very good value.

Another way to keep up to date, both in regard to varieties and the latest methods of culture, is to join the British National Carnation Society (which, of course, also caters for growers of pinks).

The lists of suggested varieties are as follows:

BORDER CARNATIONS
The following are good outdoor varieties which are also capable of taking prizes at exhibitions. The varieties noted as scented have a strong clove scent, but generally are not quite so perfect in form.

120

Alice Forbes (*also known as Alice Forbes Improved*). White, marked rose-cerise.

Beauty of Cambridge. Sulphur yellow.

Consul. Bright orange-apricot.

Fiery Cross. Brilliant scarlet, excellent form.

Catherine Glover. Clear yellow, marked scarlet.

Harmony. French grey with heavy cerise markings.

Lavender Clove. Lavender-grey, scented.

Leslie Rennison. Deep lavender, overlaid cerise, scented.

Perfect Clove. Deep crimson, scented.

Pink Pearl. Soft pink.

Robin Thain. White, marked crimson, scented.

Santa Claus. Yellow ground picotee, heavy purple edge.

Teviotdale. Rich ruby-cerise.

Zebra. Maize-yellow, marked deep crimson.

PINKS

All are double or semi-double except Daphne, which is single with waved petals. All are good garden plants, and if well grown are suitable for exhibition. All are scented to some extent, but the scent is variable in intensity and quality.

Daphne. Shrimp pink with dark eye. Single.

Doris. Salmon-pink with light red eye. Exceptionally free-flowering over a long period.

Freckles. Rose-pink, flecked scarlet.

Gaiety. Bright rose.

Laura. Deep orange-pink. Growth like Doris.

Lillian. White, very free-flowering.

London Glow. Deep maroon with white wire edge. Sometimes produces exhibition laced blooms.

London Poppet. Ground white tinged pink, laced ruby-red.

Prudence. Pale pink ground, laced dark red.

Robin. Scarlet.

Show Aristocrat. Pale Venetian pink with buff eye.

Show Beauty. Deep pink, dark crimson eye.

Show Portrait. Deep cardinal red.

Swanlake. Large white, excellent form.

Timothy. Silver-pink, flecked cerise.

Winsome. Rich crimson-pink.

PERPETUAL-FLOWERING CARNATIONS

Allwood's Crimson. Crimson.

Bailey's Delight. Pink.

Bailey's Splendour. Pink.

Bonnie Charlie. Orange.

Fragrant Ann. White.

Golden Rain. Yellow.

Joker. Crimson.

Jumbo Sim. Scarlet.

Margaret. Purple.

Northland. White.

Paris. Pink.

Viking. Cerise.

Zunessa. Mauve, variegated.

Zuni. Dark cerise, marked crimson.

Index

References in parentheses indicate line drawings in the text.

123

O
Origin of carnations, 9–10

P
Perlite, 93
Perpetual-flowering carnations,
  blooms, number of, 14
  calyx splitting, 90
  cultivation, 83–99
  disbudding, 13
  greenhouse, cold, in beds, 96–98
      planting, 97
      staking, 97
      watering, 98
    in pots, 94–96
    heated, 85–90
      cutting blooms, 90
      disbudding, (89), 88–89
      flowering times, 88–89
      potting, 85–86
      repotting, 90
      shading, 89
      staking, 88
      temperatures, 85–86, 90
      ventilation, 87–88, 90
      watering, 87
  growth of, (11), 12–14, 83–84, (84)
  hardiness, 12, 23
  origin, 12
  propagation, cuttings, 91–94, (92)
    compost for, 91, 93
    in cold greenhouse, 95–96
    rooted treatment, 93–94
    rooting, 93
    taking, 91
    watering, 94
    when to take, 14
  seed, 102
  ring culture, 98–99
  sand culture, 98
  scent, 13
  stopping, 13, 86–87, (86)
  temperatures for, 12–13, 23
  types of, 13
  varieties, 122
Pests, 105–108
  build up of, 61
pH, 29–31

Physiological disorders, 111–112
Picotees, definition of, 16
Pinks, bicolors, 18
  cultivation, 17, 22–23, 69–82
    disbudding, 71–72
    feeding, 72
    planting, (57), 71
    under glass, 81
  definition of, 16–17
  exhibiting, 18–19
  fancies, 18
  flowers, types of, 17–18
  growth of, 17
  hardiness, 23
  laced, 18
  modern, 70–73
    stopping, 79, (80), 81
  old garden, 69–70
    growth of, 70
    scent of, 81–82
    stopping, 79
  propagation, Bridesmaid, 72–73
    cuttings, 73–78, (75), (76)
      compost for, 73–74
      inserting, 77
      method, 73–74
      rooted, treatment of, 77
      slitting stems, 78
      taking, 74, 76–77
    layering, 72–73
    pipings, 78
    seed, 102–103
    slips, 78
  scent in, 17
    in modern, 81–82
  selfs, 18
  varieties, 121
Pipings, 78
Plant food, 32–39
Planting, see Annual carnations,
    Border carnations, Perpetual-
    flowering and Pinks
Potting, 50–52, (51)
    compost, 47–49
    watering after, 52–53
Propagation, see Annual carnations,
    Border carnations, Perpetual-
    flowering and Pinks